OPENINGS TO THE INFINITE OCEAN

Openings to the infinite ocean
A FRIENDLY OFFERING OF HOPE

THE 2020 SWARTHMORE LECTURE

TOM SHAKESPEARE

First published August 2020

Quaker Books, Friends House, 173 Euston Road, London NW1 2BJ

www.quaker.org.uk

Enquiries should be addressed to the Publications Manager,
Quaker Books, Friends House, 173 Euston Road, London NW1 2BJ.

© Tom Shakespeare 2020

ISBN: 978-1-9993141-8-7
eISBN: 978-1-9993141-9-4

Book design by Cox Design, Witney

THE SWARTHMORE LECTURE

The Swarthmore lectureship was established by the Woodbrooke Extension Committee at a meeting held 9 December 1907. The minute of the committee provided for an "annual lecture on some subject relating to the message and work of the Society of Friends".

The name Swarthmore was chosen in memory of the home of Margaret Fell (later Fox), which was always open to the earnest seeker after Truth, and from which Quakers were sent loving words of sympathy as well as substantial material help.

The lecture is funded by Woodbrooke Quaker Study Centre and overseen and supported by the Swarthmore Lecture Committee, which is appointed by the trustees of Woodbrooke. It is a significant part of the education work undertaken at and from Woodbrooke.

The lectureship has a twofold purpose: to interpret to the members of the Society of Friends their message and mission; and to bring before the public the spirit, aims and fundamental principles of Friends. The lecturers alone are responsible for any opinions expressed.

The lectureship provides for the delivery of a lecture, usually at the time of Britain Yearly Meeting of the Society of Friends, and for its dissemination, usually in the form of a book. Due to the public health crisis around COVID-19, the planned Yearly Meeting was postponed. Nevertheless, a lecture related to this publication was given by Tom Shakespeare on Saturday 1 August 2020 and live-streamed internationally through the Woodbrooke website.

The Swarthmore Lecture Committee can be contacted at Woodbrooke Quaker Study Centre, 1046 Bristol Road, Selly Oak, Birmingham B29 6LJ.

www.woodbrooke.org.uk/swarthmorelecture

Dedicated to my mother,
a light shining in Buckinghamshire.

ACKNOWLEDGEMENTS

Thanks to Jenny Routledge, Caro Kelly, Simon Best and the other members of the Woodbrooke Committee who first discerned that I might have something to offer, and who then faithfully supported me as I groped towards understanding what that might be. Among many Quaker scholars and educators, I benefited from the advice of Mark Russ, who generously shared his work on Jürgen Moltmann; Madeleine Pennington, who equally generously shared her work on George Keith; and Stuart Masters, who talked to me about early Quakers. I also learned from the example of Eden Grace's wonderful Swarthmore Lecture in 2019.

Other Christian thinkers and pastors whose support and advice I gratefully acknowledge include Angus Aagard, Elizabeth and Chris Oldfield, and Mark Vernon. In particular, I greatly appreciate the ideas and encouragement that Sally Phillips and John Naudé gave me on this journey.

On a return to Newcastle in November 2019, I was lucky to re-encounter friendly scholars from PEALS (the Policy, Ethics and Life Sciences Research Institute), most of whom I had first met 20 years ago. All of them offered me new leads: Simon Woods, with his knowledge of palliative care ethics; Robert Simpson, who brought his anthropologist's insight; and Robert Song, who offered me the wisdom of a moral theologian. It was a warm reunion that reminded me how sustaining the North East has always been to me, intellectually as well as socially.

A large part of this book recounts positive stories of good interventions. Thanks again to Madeleine Pennington, who suggested many of these, and also to Beverley Rose Barnett, who gave me two leads, and to my colleagues Chris Bonnell, who told me about the school anti-violence project, and Dixon Chibanda, who told me about Friendship Bench.

On a personal level, thanks to Jackie for decades of friendship and intellectual support, to Hilary and Phil for ideas and kindness, to my brother James for his wisdom and care, and to Carmen for her integrity, love and fellowship.

None of these are to blame for anything I have got wrong in this book.

CONTENTS

Let the words of my mouth and the meditation of my heart
be acceptable to you, O Lord, my rock and my redeemer.

– Psalm 19:14

See, I am making all things new.

– Revelation 21:5

INTRODUCTION

Why are we hopeless?

In our current era, where every day brings more news of global warming and extreme weather events, where everyday life is devastated by a virus, where our leaders seem collectively to have taken leave of their senses, and where populist policies and politicians are undermining peace and prosperity, it is easy to be pessimistic. There have been tough times before, but today everything looks extremely gloomy.

Traditional believers had hope in the Second Coming of Christ, and then after that they had hope in the Afterlife. Following the Enlightenment in the 18th century, people had hope in the moral progress of human society: absolute rulers were giving way to constitutional monarchies and knowledge was replacing superstition. Then the industrial revolution seemed to promise the scientific reorganisation of society and better health and prosperity. But the 20th-century evils of genocide and Stalinism dislodged this optimism, and many people realised that modernity might just mean better ways of killing and enslaving people: as Theodor Adorno (1951) famously said, "To write a poem after Auschwitz is barbaric."

In the decades after World War II, Western countries enjoyed economic prosperity and a measure of consensus, built around full employment and the welfare state. Democracy seemed to have solved the problem – or at least the economic ideas of John Maynard Keynes had. But this gave way to political turmoil, oil crisis and 'stagflation' in the 1970s. The new orthodoxy of the 1980s onwards was based on market fundamentalism, deregulation of the financial sector and the acceptance of inequality by both Right and Left. Both sides felt that economic growth could 'trickle down' from the rich to benefit the poor, who would be better off than they would otherwise have been. From the mid-1990s, the New Labour version modified this basic assumption to add redistributive measures such as progressive taxation and tax credits. As Peter Mandelson said in 1998, "We are intensely relaxed about people getting filthy rich, as long as they pay their taxes."

Today, the gamble on market fundamentalism appears to have been lost. The remorseless logic of capitalism means that industries in Europe and America are often 'off-shored', so that production heads to low- and middle-income countries, which pay cheaper wages. Increasing numbers of jobs for both blue collar and now white collar workers are being lost through automation and AI (artificial intelligence). Many are exploiting themselves in the gig economy. Even in academia, where I work, numerous junior staff are suffering unfair conditions that resemble the 'freelance' approach of the Uber driver. My step-daughter, who has just earned a PhD, has far more difficult prospects than the ones I faced 25 years ago. Across the whole economy, while employment rates are high, many do not have a good, steady, well-paying job. As a result, many working families are reliant on welfare benefits.

Inequality in UK society increased greatly in the 1980s, and as of 2017 the UK was one of the most unequal societies in the world, 32nd out of 40 countries in terms of the Gini coefficient of income equality (post-tax and transfers) according to the Organisation for Economic Co-operation and Development (OECD, 2020). Life expectancy growth rates are levelling off, especially for middle-aged men (Raleigh, 2019). Younger generations, saddled with student debt, are finding it very hard to match the prosperity of their parents, let alone invest in a home of their own. In a YouGov poll of social attitudes quoted in the *Financial Times* in May 2019, 85 per cent of the British public believed that a fairer society would offer more to people who had greater talents and worked harder (Giles, 2019).

The response of many who feel excluded by society and abandoned by an economy that no longer wants or values them is to turn to populism. Returns to nationalism and protectionism can be seen in anti-EU sentiment in the UK; the Far Right in France, Germany and Italy; the 'strong man' regimes of Hungary, Russia and Turkey; and most influentially the Trump administration. Many prefer to blame the elites, the establishment or foreigners for their problems. Nor is truth widely respected: 'fake news' and other forms of media manipulation have proliferated, right up to outright lying, which appears more acceptable today than ever before. Even science is challenged by 'anti-vaxxers' and others. All of this is very depressing to anyone who hopes for less conflict, greater equality and more truth in politics.

Looking more widely at the world, we do not live in peaceful times. The conflict in the Middle East appears to be irresolvable and only getting worse, thanks to President Trump and Prime Minister

Netanyahu. Rivalry between Iran and Saudi Arabia has resulted in bloody proxy wars in Lebanon and Yemen. Afghanistan, Iraq and Syria appear not to have benefited from Western intervention.

When I read the testimony of our forebears in *Quaker faith & practice*, what most depresses me is that we have had many of the same problems for generation after generation. So, for example, Joseph Rowntree said in 1904, "The soup kitchen in York never has difficulty in obtaining financial aid, but an enquiry into the extent and causes of poverty would enlist little support" (*Quaker faith & practice*, 23.18). I could cite the British Yearly Meeting statement in 1987 about polarisation between the haves and the have-nots (*Quaker faith & practice*, 23.21), or the 1992 statement about homelessness (*Quaker faith & practice*, 23.23). The poor are always with us (Matthew 26:11).

But what might be new is realisation of the environmental crisis we face. Unrestrained market fundamentalism has been unwilling to factor in public goods such as environmental protection. Sea levels are rising. Temperature is rising. More extreme weather events are following, with all the deaths, dislocations and refugee movements that they bring in their wake. Species are facing extinction. Plastic waste is accumulating in natural sanctuaries. There certainly seem to be signs of hope: renewable energy, electric cars, more public transport. Yet I picked up a book from the Quaker library at Woodbrooke that was called exactly that, *Signs of hope* (Starke, 1990). This was an update of the World Commission on Environment and Development's report in 1987, *Our common future*. I found it depressing to read that today's concern about the planet is far from new: almost everything important about the environment had been said in 1987, more than 30 years ago. Undoubtedly some significant changes had resulted, but the overall picture remains very bad. In 2019, the Oxford Word of the Year was 'climate emergency' (Oxford Languages, 2019). No wonder Greta Thunberg has said:

> Adults keep saying we owe it to the young people, to give them hope. But I don't want your hope. *I don't want you to be hopeful. I want you to panic.* I want you to feel the fear I feel every day. I want you to act. I want you to act as you would in

a crisis. I want you to act as if the house is on fire, because it is. (quoted in NPR, 2019)

Many young people today feel this desperation that Thunberg highlights. Older generations may have a different stake in climate change. But many of us have children and grandchildren. All of us have a stake in creation.

I disagree with Greta Thunberg's implication about hope. Hope is not the same as optimism. It is not a Panglossian confidence that all will be for the best in the best of all possible worlds. To have hope is not to expect a better future. We can be fearful and yet hopeful. We have to take action to bring about a better outcome.

As Quakers, we still rely on the virtues of trust, solidarity, toleration, and compromise. We have our testimonies to peace, truth, equality, and simplicity. We have our social witness. But are these enough in practice? Does an emergency not demand more of us? Where can we find hope when everything looks dark?

This book is a humble and often very personal offering of hope. Not all of it will speak to all readers. Chapter 1 explores the beliefs and practices of early Quakers, to whom I strive to be faithful and from whom I think we can learn. Chapter 2 explores hope itself, drawing mainly on the Bible but also on the theology of Jürgen Moltmann. Chapter 3 offers ways of looking for hope and places to find it. There is quite a lot about disability in this chapter. I have not looked for the good works initiated by Quaker meetings, although I know there are very many of those. The final chapter gives some hopeful suggestions about ways of acting in the world. The book was written before the COVID-19 pandemic and edited as the full effects were being felt worldwide. On the plus side, responses to the virus have revealed the hopeful, helpful actions of thousands of neighbours and health workers. On the minus side, they have also revealed the hopelessness of many living in fear, amid rumours and suspicions of authority, and the selfishness of some. But, while the virus may highlight both problems and solutions, it does not change the fundamental equation.

I am a Christian. I know some Quakers would not say that of themselves, or use the 'God' word. These readers might be uncomfortable with chapters 1 and 2. Please bear with me, because I trust that you will find something useful to your Quakerism, if you can see beyond my language. I also hope that Christian readers who are not Quakers will find value in these chapters: I think that the Quaker tradition, which I take to be one of mysticism allied to social action, can speak to an important need in contemporary faith communities. Regardless of your beliefs, I hope that chapters 3 and 4 might speak to your condition and offer some ways forward.

CHAPTER 1

Let your life preach

It is perhaps hard to imagine today, but there have certainly been moments in human history when it seemed that the Kingdom of God was at hand. One such moment is described in the New Testament, in particular in the Acts of the Apostles and the Epistles. Paul burns with missionary enthusiasm as he travels around the ancient world. Those early Christians must have been a very intense people. They were living in expectation of the Second Coming of Christ (Parousia) and the end times. This phase lasted for a few centuries, and then the institutionalisation of Christianity took over. The Nicene Creed was agreed in AD 325. Emperor Constantine converted to Christianity on his deathbed in 337. The church became an institution. There were squabbles. The Western and Eastern churches split in 1054. The early promise was lost.

A thousand years or so after that first window of oneness, I want to identify another moment, represented by Francis of Assisi (1181–1226). Francis, son of nobility, came to throw away all of the division that had come before him, to reform his religion, to tread in the footsteps of Christ, and to preach unity with creation. He set out to restore the message of Jesus, which led him to care for the poor and the sick, whom he saw also had that of God in them. His friars challenged the established church to go out and live the Gospel. I have an Italian film by Roberto Rossellini – *Francis, God's jester* – about Francis and his followers rediscovering the primitive Christianity of the Gospels, running joyously through the fields, and loving Brother Ox and Brother Ass. This is the saint who first created the Nativity scene of the holy child worshipped by the animals. A saying commonly attributed to Francis is, "Preach the Gospel at all times and if necessary use words." This doesn't seem far to me from "Let your lives preach."

Of course there have been many other such moments of return to simplicity and to the primitive Christianity of the desert fathers – Benedict of Nursia (480–547), John Wycliffe (1320s–1384), Ignatius of Loyola (1491–1556) and Teresa of Ávila (1515–1584). In other traditions, the Buddha and many, many others have said similar things about peace, love and unity. After all, the mystical vision – the pure vision – is one that most religions share at their core, as Father Richard Rohr (2019) has said.

The history that interests us most here is the moment in 1647 when along came George Fox, seeking a new intimacy with God and preaching a simple Christianity. Fox, like Francis, rejected his comfortable background and did something radically different. The intensity of his charismatic vision, coupled with his genius for organisation, led to the growth of the Religious Society of Friends in the 1650s and its consolidation during the rest of the century.

Following Ben Pink Dandelion, Stuart Masters, Mark Russ, and other Quaker historians and theologians, it seems to me that these early Quakers roaming the countryside were very like those early Christians. Quakers were Christians because they could confidently match their experiences to those they found in the Bible, not because they were doctrinally exact. They felt that existing churches taught a husk, not the vital life at the heart of religion. They believed they had the same presence of Christ in their lives as the early Christians had. They were not simply mimicking 1st-century followers of Jesus.

These early Quakers were quite ordinary people in extraordinary circumstances, preaching the coming Kingdom of God. They had an apocalyptic vision – a revelation of how things should be – which they put into practice as the best way to act out their faith. They not only expected the end of the world but also acted to create the reality of heaven on earth (Dandelion et al., 1998: 126). Quakerism was not about logic or reasoning, but a deep, heartful sense of unity with God. It was the same deep conviction that had struck Paul on the road to Damascus and connected those other early Christians in the years after Jesus had been crucified. Early Quakerism was Pauline Christianity revived, right down to the persecution. Even Quaker worship, the silent waiting on the Spirit, draws on what Paul wrote about. Jesus had said, "For where two or three are gathered in my name, I am there among them" (Matthew 18:20). Paul said, "Do you not know that you are God's temple and that God's Spirit dwells in you?" (1 Corinthians 3:16). Later he said:

Let two or three prophets speak, and let the others weigh what is said. If a revelation is made to someone else sitting nearby, let the first person be silent. For you can all prophesy

one by one, so that all may learn and all be encouraged.
(1 Corinthians 14:29–31)

I am sure that early Christians, gathering in private houses, were
waiting on the Spirit in the same way as we Quakers have done for
350 years, although I hope we are doing so in a more inclusive way
than Paul could imagine.

The writings of these early Quakers demonstrate how they felt
they had rediscovered early Christianity as expressed in the Acts of
the Apostles. Robert Barclay wrote:

> When I came into the silent assemblies of God's people, I felt
> a secret power among them, which touched my heart; and as
> I gave way unto it I found the evil weakening in me and the
> good raised up. (*Quaker faith & practice* 19.21)

So too William Penn talks about "wholly dying to the world and
being made conformable to the will of God" (Penn, 1801: 31).
Rather than emphasising Original Sin, as the Puritans did, Quakers
preached that freedom from sin was possible in this life and that
God was guiding their actions. It was what Douglas Gwyn calls an
"apocalyptic spirituality", combining the intimate and the ultimate
(Dandelion et al., 1998: 118).

These true Christian mystics experienced the Kingdom of God.
They felt they were living the truth, free of sin, redeemed by Christ
and sanctified by the Light within – that of God reflected in them.
They were an incendiary force within British society. By 1657,
around 1,000 of them were in prison for this preaching. Quakers
were heralds of this coming Kingdom.

As Gerald Hewitson told us in his 2013 Swarthmore Lecture,
early Friends spoke from a belief that the values of the real world
were false. Many of us would nod in agreement today. He quoted
Edward Burrough:

> We are not for names, nor men, nor titles of government,
> nor are we for this party or against the other... but we are
> for justice and mercy and truth and peace and true freedom,

that these may be exalted in our nation. (*Quaker faith & practice* 23.11)

But I think today we are happier with this political positioning that we might be with some of the primitive Christianity that underpins it. Isaac Penington is one of my favourite writers among those early Quakers because of that quotation which begins, "Our life is love and peace and tenderness and bearing one with another" (*Quaker faith & practice* 10.01). However, he also wrote:

> Give over thine own willing, give over thy own running, give over thine own desiring to know or be anything and sink down to the seed which God sows in the heart, and let that grown in thee and be in thee and breathe in thee and act in thee; and thou shalt find by sweet experience that the Lord knows that and loves and owns that, and will lead it to the inheritance of Life, which is its portion. (*Quaker faith & practice* 26.70)

This mystical injunction to obedience to God, indeed unity with God, reminds us how very Biblical and Christian these early Quakers were, and perhaps how much we have lost in the modern liberal Quaker movement. Then, Quakers had all the mysticism of the Catholic tradition, together with the outrageous certainty that they could know God directly and hear the voice of God in their contemplative form of worship. As Margaret Fell famously recorded George Fox preaching in Ulverston in 1652:

> You will say, Christ saith this, and the apostles say this, but what canst thou say? Art thou a child of Light and hast walked in the Light, and what thou speakest is it inwardly from God? (*Quaker faith & practice* 19.07)

That's an extraordinary way of challenging an audience. No wonder the Puritans would beat up these heretical Quakers or throw them into prison. But I think it's very nearly the same thing that Joan of

Arc said, and Francis said, and Teresa of Ávila said, along with every Christian mystic who has felt a deep personal connection with the Divine, or indeed Sufi mystics or Hindu mystics.

Importantly, for the early Quakers – as for the early Christians – this injunction to seek unity with God was closely connected to a belief that the Second Coming of Christ was at hand. Many nonconformist believers in the mid-17th century felt this: they were sweeping away unimportant aspects of Christianity in preparation for the Last Days. But after the Restoration of Charles II in 1660, Quakers retreated into Quietism, putting the Parousia aside and abandoning eschatology. Robert Barclay and William Penn ensured the theological coherence and continuity of Quakers by maintaining their forms of religious practice – silent waiting upon God, no clergy and no sacraments (Dandelion et al., 1998).

There are certainly contemporary Quaker thinkers who are developing Quaker theology. But, as a body, Quakers now seem rather atheological. When I became an attender with the Religious Society of Friends in Newcastle in January 1997, I soon discovered it was not quite polite to ask Quakers what they believed. I could see what Quakers did, and I admired it: the injunction faithfully followed to "let your life speak"; the personal integrity; the commitment to peace, poverty alleviation or other social justice causes; the silent waiting upon God; the lack of creed, sacrament or liturgy. Newcastle Friends such as Geoffrey and Rachel Cundall, Ellie Earnshaw, Grigor McClelland, Douglas and Sarah Rennie, Joan and Bryce Robson, and Jackie Leach Scully were inspirational to me. I joined the Society due to their example. From a family of nonconformists, I had been born an Anglican, fallen away from all Christianity for a decade, immersed myself in left-wing politics, and later explored Buddhist meditation. The Quakers, with their freedom, silent worship and social radicalism, were just the stepping-stone I needed back into organised religion. For me as an Englishman, it felt like Zen for the English.

To me, Liberal Quakers seemed to be religious humanists, for the most part – a worthy congregation of like-minded, mainly middle-class and white people who did their best to be good, and to do good, and were notably tolerant of LGBT folk. Their testimonies were all about truth, equality, simplicity, and peace: in other words, there was a lot more practice than faith, and it suited me. Quakers did not tend to talk much about God. No wonder that my Anglican mother wondered whether I was a Christian at all. In contrast to those who said one could be 'spiritual but not religious', I maintained that one should be 'religious but not spiritual', which to my mind subsumed most Quakers, quite a few Anglicans and many liberal Jews.

Quaker faith & practice helpfully tells us, "It is not necessary that we should know all mysteries before we begin to follow Christ" (20.19). And I am sure this is so. But we need to work actively on the life within, and I wonder how seriously we all still practise this. In my Quaker worship, I found that Jesus was lacking, except as an example of a good life and sensible preaching, and Christ was lacking, in the sense of any focus on incarnation or redemption (Russ, 2019; Ward, 2019). There was a sidelining of the Bible: "Scripture has little, if any corporate function" (Russ, 2019: 31). Indeed, it is quite possible to be a Quaker deist or a Quaker atheist. In 2013, only 37 per cent of Quakers regarded themselves as Christian (Hampton, 2014). Ben Pink Dandelion (2014) reminds us that mostly we believe in the Absolute Perhaps.

The core of the contemporary Quakerism that I encountered was the practice of silent waiting upon God, rather than an affiliation with a Christian path, in particular. I think the fact that we have many attenders who do not make the next move to become members of the Society is testament to this: sitting in silence weekly is a rather minimal commitment (Dandelion et al., 1998: 191). In a Quaker meeting, the practice is primary, due to what Ben Pink Dandelion has called "the sacralisation of silence" (Dandelion et al., 1998: 180). The lack of explicit 'belief-talk' perhaps means that we can better defend ourselves against the rational atheism of Richard Dawkins and his followers. But it also means that we might be individually lost.

Rather than working towards the Kingdom of God, and considering how to bring that about, we live in the Eternal Now, as *Quaker faith & practice* counsels:

"For us it is not so important when the perfect world will be achieved or what it will be like. What matters is living our lives in the power of love and not worrying too much about the results... We must literally not take too much thought for the morrow but throw ourselves whole-heartedly into the present." (*Quaker faith & practice* 24.60)

In Mark Russ's (2019: 34) memorable phrase, we are a pilgrim people without a destination. Maybe, following Mark Russ, Ben Pink Dandelion and other Quakers, we would be better off trying to rediscover the confidence of early Friends, looking to:

The dynamic, active hope of a God who both meets us in the present moment and draws us forward to a Christ-shaped future, whose story provides a framework for making sense of the Quaker experience, and whose character sets the boundaries within which we are free to enact God's Kingdom in unexpected ways, is always available to us. (Russ, 2019: 47)

What changed my own thinking was reading the Bible. My great-grandfather, a Baptist minister who was the son of a Baptist minister, grew up in a house with only two books: the Bible and *Pilgrim's progress*. My grandfather could recite much of the Bible from memory. I did know many scripture stories from school, but I had never read it cover to cover. Now, at a friend's encouragement, I set out to read one chapter each from the Old and New Testaments every day, together with a psalm or a section of Proverbs. My friend told me: if you read the Bible every day and finish it, you will end up a born-again Christian. I scoffed at her. But I must have silently absorbed the messages, some of which were incomprehensible or nonsensical, but many of which were meaningful, and all of which worked away at my soul. On my birthday, 11 May 2018, I read the passage from the New Testament aloud. It was the tenth chapter of John:

Jesus answered, "I have told you, and you do not believe. The works that I do in my Father's name testify to me; but you

do not believe, because you do not belong to my sheep. My
sheep hear my voice. I know them, and they follow me. (John
10:25–27)

I realised I was the one who had heard the message but had not
believed. And in that moment, my eyes filled with tears and I was
born again into that "Christ-shaped future". I have been weeping
ever since.

Everyone has their own path, but I ended up feeling that
Quakers needed to remember God, not imagine that they could do
very well without. It was this that could give us a sense of what we
are here for, why we are sitting in silence, why Quakers still have
a vital purpose, as the Christian mystics we surely are or can be.
We might inspire the busy, noisy practices of our neighbouring faith
communities, and offer a way back to God for the secular, soul-less
peoples among whom we live and work. Early Quakers often said,
"We preach Christ crucified." Today, I think even more importantly,
we could preach God incarnated among us – the desolating, jolting
presence of the Light born again every day, in our own hearts and in
our neighbourhoods.

Quakers are fond of saying, "Let your life speak." I have watched
with admiration how very many Quakers set up foodbanks and
night-shelters, or keep those found guilty of child sex offences
within circles of support and accountability, or promote restorative
justice, or work quietly for peace in troubled parts of the world, or
drive ambulances in wartime, or campaign against the arms trade.
All of these actions are undoubtedly and admirably "letting one's
life speak". These and other examples were among the reasons I
joined the Society, although I have never done anything so brave or
dedicated.

But originally, the phrase was different. It was "let your life
preach," as George Fox wrote from Launceston Jail in 1656 (Fox,
1831: epistle 200). It's not just about doing good works, vital though
that undoubtedly is. We are called to be patterns and examples,
just as the Apostles were. But the early Quakers would surely
have considered that the role of a Friend was to enable God to be
manifested through themselves. I take George Fox to have been

saying, "You are the people who have been called to gather everyone into this new experience. The very way you live your life, the way you live with other people, will communicate that." This was a statement about the mission of early Friends. They needed to be visibly different, and to communicate something by the nature of their lives, by the biblically based life they were leading. I think this is a little more than simply leading an admirable life.

James Naylor took this to an extreme with his belief that each person has to achieve again in his or her own person Christ's external story lived through the individual – complete with a cycle of healing, teaching, dying, and being born again. And hope plays its part in Naylor's thinking:

> There is a spirit which I feel that delights to do no evil, nor to revenge any wrong, but delights to endure all things, in hope to enjoy its own in the end. (*Quaker faith & practice* 19.12)

This was not simply a matter of belief, but of revelation, of Christ being revealed to him. This spirit of Christ enabled Naylor to endure suffering and persecution. In a less demonstrative sense, Paul tells us in Galatians 2:20 that "it is no longer I who live, but it is Christ who lives in me". So for the early Quakers, "the light in people's consciences was nothing less than the presence of the risen and returned Christ" (Dandelion et al., 1998: 102). Christianity is a gift that we get, a combination of fearlessness, hope and conviction that comes from something happening to us that is not within our control. As George Fox said: "All things were new, and all creation gave another smell unto me than before, beyond what words can utter" (Fox, 1952: 27).

No wonder this visceral Christianity was blasphemous for Protestants. Early Quakers were outrageous to respectable society, for example by promoting the spiritual equality of women. They were charismatic, they were prophetic, but all based on what they read in the Bible. Theirs was a process of group spiritual discernment. They thought they had discovered something that was the solution to everything that had gone wrong.

In 2020, Quakers are typical of our neighbours: we like to be different, but not very different. We are uncomfortable with evangelism. We would rather others found us by happenstance than we went out and spoke to them directly. Douglas Gwyn says that "we have traded quiescence for toleration, quaintness for respect, acculturation for renewal, we have traded a covenant for a contract" (Dandelion et al., 1998: 137). We certainly lead simpler, less materialistic lives. We volunteer, we campaign, we read *The Friend* or at least *The Guardian*. We work for peace and justice. But are we letting our lives preach?

Quakers have this wonderful resource in our history, and we should draw on it fully. This is a different way of doing evangelism. I want to suggest that letting your life preach is not about your own effort. It might require letting go of the attempt to be a good person, step aside as an ego, and being open to God working through you. Richard Rohr says:

> The theological virtue of hope is the patient and trustful willingness to live without closure, without resolution, and still be content and even happy because our Satisfaction is now at another level, and our Source is beyond ourselves. (Rohr, n.d.)

"Looking for that of God in everyone" is not about everyone being a bit wonderful. It is about everyone being a vessel for God to act through. Unless the creature allows itself to be a vessel through which the creator can act, the creature is not living what it is meant to be. As early Quakers thought, there is a source of guidance and transformation available to everyone, if only we surrender to it and turn to it. There is a Light that would transform everything. What prevents us taking advantage of it? We can make every moment an opportunity for transformation.

In particular, I believe that our silence is a gift, a mystical gift, which we can share with all Christians, and others who have different faiths or are looking for meaning because they have none. We have sacralised silence. I have been to many Christian churches of different denominations. There is much there that we lack as

Quakers: the prayer, the singing, the Bible, the sacraments. But there is also much noise, much bustle, much chaos. Moments of silence are very, very few. The still small voice of calm, which the Bible talks about and which Quaker worship embodies, is often lacking.

I think we can rediscover hope in that silence. There is an almost undetectable hum of love underneath the noise, if we can only turn off our phones, put aside our chores, centre down, and feel it, together. I think people in this overwhelming, materialistic 21st century need to find a mystical unity with God, even though they may not know it yet. They don't have to call this "God". They can call it Inner Light, or peace, or calm, or mindfulness, or whatever gets them through. They can seek unity with the Universe, or Eternity, or Nature or anything they like. But it is all about slowing down, stopping and letting Reality in.

For I think that life is like living in a house. Your dwelling has different rooms. One is about issues intellectual. Another is about things emotional. There should be a room for activities physical. And the last is for matters spiritual. When you have a house, you do not spend equal amounts of time in all the rooms. You probably have a favourite room. But if you never went into one of your rooms, it would surely be odd. You would be closing yourself off from an important experience. You would not be deriving the full benefit of this wonderful house that is yours. I think too many people never go into the room that is about the Spirit (Chaplin, 2008). They lack this aspect in their everyday. Or perhaps they feel they can compensate by buying more things, going on more holidays, having better food and drink, or spending more time at the gym or the cinema or the theatre. But these things are merely decorative, compared to the fundamental things in life. Quakers might say: we have a room for you. Come and sit in silence for a while with us. Find hope. Be refreshed in the Spirit, and leave knowing more about your purpose on this earth.

But maybe we have to accept that silence is not enough. Quakerism is not simply an exercise in meditation. "Silence, and absence of religious forms, are not in themselves religious" (Dandelion et al., 1998: 192). If you want to practise mindfulness, this will undoubtedly be good for you, but we do more than that here. Silence is a way, not a destination. Many of us are not simply religious humanists. We are in the tradition of George Fox and those other early Friends (Ward, 2019).

We believe that all of life can be sacramental. In the words of Edgar Dunstan, quoted in *Quaker faith & practice*, "we are all humble learners in the school of Christ" (11.18). We are waiting on God, not just on the final handshake that says we have done our hour of quiet. "Seek to know each other in matters which are eternal," *Advices & queries* (1.02.19) also tell us. This is mysticism, in the sense of a direct relationship with God. Rachel Muers (2015) says it is more important to be truthful and faithful to the leading than to worry about whether you are going to be successful. Let God worry about the implications. This is hard, and sometimes frustrating, particularly in a world full of distractions.

And outside our meetings for worship, what to do? I think a good question might be to ask: what would make us, as Friends, really unpopular today? As Quakers it seems to me that we need to be a constant disturbance in society. We need to be a troubling people. Maybe we are called to do just that. We need to listen to God, and then act according to what his Word – or, if you prefer, to what our conscience – demands. We should not let hope be overcome by fear. Here there is a tension between what we might call Quaker spirituality, which says we won't get there unless we stop doing and surrender to God, and an activist mentality which says that we have to do it ourselves and that waiting to be led is an excuse for not doing anything.

I believe that both are badly needed. If we are going to be more like the early Quakers, who preached the equality of women and said they listened directly to God, maybe we should be more outrageous to respectable society. We can be among those disciplined nonconformists whom Martin Luther King saw as the hope for a secure and liveable world. We can be more than *Guardian* readers!

CHAPTER 2

Faith, hope and love

The author of that medieval classic of spirituality *The cloud of unknowing* says:

> God is incomprehensible to the intellect… Nobody's mind
> is powerful enough to grasp who God is. We can only know
> God by experiencing God's love. (Butcher, 2009: 12)

I hope this is a sentiment that George Fox would have understood. I find it both challenging and helpful to be reminded that it is not always the brain that we need. I think that modern Friends are comfortable with anything intellectual, but not always as willing to wait on love. Maybe this is a problem with the Western tradition of Christianity. The Eastern church is much readier to understand that we approach God with our heart, not with our mind. Belief is not a rational thing. It is an openness to love. As Rowan Williams (2012) has said, to talk of God is like falling in love.

The two central moments in the Christian liturgical year are Christmas and Easter. Both these great festivals – like other dates, such as Ascension and Pentecost – are about hope and they are also about love. The birth of the Christ Child is quite obviously about hope for the world. Every birth is hope incarnate. Love has come into the world: 'Immanuel' means 'God with us'. The incarnation of God, God becoming flesh and living among us, if we take it literally, is an extraordinary thing.

The death and resurrection of Jesus are also about hope for the world, because if we have faith, it gives us hope. The theology of 'penal substitutionism' – the sacrifice that God pays to redeem us – may not speak to our condition. To me, it makes more sense as a plot twist in *The lion, the witch and the wardrobe* than it does as theology. With Richard Rohr, I would rather concentrate on Jesus as "God's perfect and utterly free initiative of love" (Rohr, 2016: 197). But the Crucifixion is still centrally important to our Christianity, as symbolism of redemptive suffering. Where there is the greatest evil, there is also the greatest good. It is about overcoming adversity, about how even the worst fate in the world is something that can be survived and about how hope revives despite apparent defeat. There is an ocean of light that overcomes the darkness. The message lives on. "We preach Christ crucified," said the early Quakers.

Friends may not celebrate these dates, but other Christians do, and they bring comfort to millions of people around the world. I think it is sad that Quakers have lost those moments of hope in our annual cycles. But we are making a huge claim in dispensing with the liturgical calendar. We are saying that we do not need reminders or symbolism, because we live them out all the time. It is incumbent on us to experience Christmas and Easter every day.

What might this mean? I think Francis Spufford helped me to understand in his wonderful book *Unapologetic* (2012). God comes into the world in all our joys, and dies with our failures every day. Christmas and Easter are only reminders of that. If we don't think we need reminders, then we had better be very good at living this very human cycle of hope and renewal.

In the first letter to the Corinthians, Paul famously speaks of faith, hope and charity – the last of which William Tyndale translated as love, although he was scorned by Thomas More for using such a common word (Robinson, 2015: 19). No one would dispute the importance of love. Indeed, it seems to be the central message of Christianity. In the new heaven and new earth, love will remain but there will be no need for hope. But for now, and the foreseeable future, what is the difference between faith and hope? If we have faith, why do we need hope?

Paul provides an answer in Romans, the crux of his theology:

> Therefore, since we are justified by faith, we have peace with God through our Lord Jesus Christ, through whom we have obtained access to this grace in which we stand; and we boast in our hope of sharing the glory of God. (Romans 5:1–2)

Because we have faith, we can hope for a good ending to our story. And then Paul homes in on that concept of hope:

> For in hope we were saved. Now hope that is seen is not hope. For who hopes for what is seen? But if we hope for what we do not see, we wait for it with patience. (Romans 8:24–25)

What's going on here is the sense of an ending, as the literary critic Frank Kermode has it. The ending helps us make sense of the whole thing, because we have faith:

> But, in accordance with his promise, we wait for new heavens and a new earth, where righteousness is at home. (2 Peter 3:13)

In Jürgen Moltmann's theology of hope, the ending is the Light within which we see everything else:

> Without faith's knowledge of Christ, hope becomes a utopia and remains hanging in the air. But without hope, faith falls to pieces, becomes a fainthearted and ultimately a dead faith. It is through faith that man finds the path of true life, but it is only hope that keeps him on that path. Thus it is that faith in Christ gives hope its assurance. (Moltmann, 1967: 209)

Hope and optimism are different things. Optimism is the belief that things will be better in the future; it is a cognitive belief. Hope is a quality of spirit, a feeling, something more existential. We can have hope even if we are not optimistic. We would not be talking about hope if it were easy to generate for ourselves. I think hope is a gift, often something we receive when we surrender absolutely, not something we generate ourselves. That phrase "the gift of hope" is hugely potent, as if the two words were inextricably linked in our consciousness.

Most people in the world spend their time hoping for better days, or hoping that in the end all will be well. Because we do not see very far ahead, we require faith – faith in the uncertain future – in order to remain steadfast in the dark times. Faith is like trust. It is reassurance that all will be well. Faith keeps us going when everything seems dark. Faith endures when we can't imagine how things could be better. Faith gives us the courage to take the next step. It is closely related to Grace, the understanding that whatever we can do ourselves, it is nothing compared to what God can – and will – do. We have faith that God will save us in the end, not least from ourselves, through his grace. We do not earn this salvation. Nothing we do by our own efforts could ever be enough. Grace is a gift. This was the great insight of the Protestant Reformation, but it was there originally in the writings of Paul.

Here we might turn to the medieval mystic Julian of Norwich, famously an anchoress in a cell of a church in that city. Her most famous saying is a consolation to many people who have never read her visions. I have said it more often than the advice of any other mystic, to myself and to many friends:

> All shall be well, and all shall be well, and all manner of thing shall be well. (Julian of Norwich, 1980: 99)

In this potent medieval expression of hope, we can see that Julian of Norwich has this traditional faith in God. She believes in God's grace, as Paul did before her. This is also the case when she experiences her famous vision of the nut:

> And in this he shewed me a little thing, the quantity of a hazel nut, lying in the palm of my hand, as it seemed. And it was as round as any ball. I looked upon it with the eye of my understanding, and thought, "What may this be?" And it was answered generally thus, "It is all that is made." I marvelled how it might last, for I thought it might suddenly have fallen to nothing for littleness. And I was answered in my understanding: It lasts and ever shall, for God loves it. And so have all things their beginning by the love of God. (Julian of Norwich, 1980: 10)

I cherish this vision, because it seems almost like a metaphorical expression of cosmology or theoretical physics. The nut image could be an acknowledgement of the frailty of creation – the balance of strong and weak forces that keeps everything in balance and order, the anthropocentric idea that earth is exactly the right size and in exactly the right place in the galaxy to enable creation to come into being. But for Julian, of course, this whole marvellous cosmic creation is sustained by God's love, just as it was for Paul, as we've seen:

> And now faith, hope, and love abide, these three; and the greatest of these is love. (1 Corinthians 13)

Paul wants us to live the same kind of life that Christ did, to live in the same intimacy with God that he had. George Fox shared this vision of God's grace; in despair at the state of the world in 1647, he wrote these words in his *Journal*:

> I saw also that there was an ocean of darkness and death, but an infinite ocean of light and love which flowed over the ocean of darkness. And in that also I saw the infinite love of God; and I had great openings. (*Quaker faith & practice* 19:03)

A little over 300 years later and across the Atlantic, Dr Martin Luther King said something very similar in reference to the struggle for civil rights and equality that he led: we must "accept the finite disappointment and yet cling to the infinite hope" (King, 1962). I am sure he was thinking of Paul's words, as he imagined the Apostle in his prison cell in Rome. He shared this hope for better days that lie beyond the horizon, based on his faith in God. Like early Quakers, he was motivated by the truth, which we should understand not as a series of propositions but as an inward condition of the heart, as Gerald Hewitson described it in the 2013 Swarthmore Lecture (Hewitson, 2013).

For Jürgen Moltmann, the Bible is about God's promise to his people that they will be saved in the end. In this thinking, eschatology – what is believed about the future – is the key to the Christian faith: "the glow that suffuses everything here in the dawn of an expected new day" (Moltmann, 1967: 16). In Mark Russ's words, "The anticipated future impacts on the present through the energising, active hope it inspires" (Russ, 2019: 11). If we do not have hope, all we are left with is boredom, cynicism, resignation, meaninglessness, and irony.

But many people do not have this faith, including many Quakers. We may not trust to God's grace. We may replace God's grace with the onward march of labour, or the scientific materialism of Marx, or a generalised faith in progress. However, we are more likely to find in the postmodern era that all explanatory metanarratives are rejected. People do not believe that we are going anywhere in particular. History is meaningless. God is no longer the author of the world, any more than dialectical materialism is the engine of history, or liberalism the promise of the future. There is no future to be hoped for, let alone the Parousia of Christ's return. We are in an eternal present and nothing better can be envisaged. The Old and New Testaments, most of which hope for deliverance, become unreliable, or metaphorical stories of personal, individual transformations, not collective, corporate ones.

This is one reason why I don't like the phrase 'going forward'. To me, it suggests that the future will be the same as the present: it's just more of the same, nothing but the present, infinitely extended. It implies pessimism. The big problems cannot be solved. We can expect no better. The future has been colonised by the pessimists. George Orwell (1949: 267) said, "If you want a vision of the future, imagine a boot stamping on a human face – forever." But today, it would be more like the brief apocalyptic vision in Cormack McCarthy's *The road* (2006). I would like to say 'in the future' because it is a temporal concept. I cherish the hope that the future will be very different from today. All social reformers think in this way. They have to. Martin Luther King (1963) told his audience, "We are not satisfied, and we will not be satisfied until justice rolls down like waters and righteousness like a mighty stream," and then a little later he said the immortal words "I have a dream," following which he repeated that phrase ten times. And this vision of the future was as much about the Bible as it was about American civil rights. We need visions like this, now more than ever.

Otherwise, all we are really left with is the secular version of hope, which is little more than optimism without certainty. Hope is always looking forward. However, hope for the future is based on what has happened in the past. The Jewish Marxist Walter Benjamin had a particular view of hope, bringing together past, present and future. This vision is summarised by Hirokazu Miyazaki (2004: 139): "Hope is inherited from the past, and the pull of hope in the present derives from anticipation of fulfilment contained in the past hope." The hope we need is a method. Hope in the present points to its own future moment of salvation: "Moments of hope can only be apprehended as sparks… The sparks provide a simulated view of the moments of hope as they fade away" (Miyazaki, 2004: 24).

We have the record of past times and how virtue triumphed in the end. We have evidence that things were not always like this, and we hope that change is going to come. As Paul said of Abraham, "Hoping against hope, he believed" (Romans 4:18). As a Quaker, I sit silently in worship with thousands of others. As we sit, waiting for guidance, our worship is all about hope. It is also about now, the immanence of God in the present moment. It can be about the future too: our hope that we will be given answers, even when we can't frame the right question. I love that great Quaker phrase, "Proceed as the way opens." As Ludwig Wittgenstein wrote in *Philosophical investigations*, there is no "last house in the road" (Wittgenstein, 1958: 29). We could always build another one. And so we shall. We are putting our trust in God – or the Universe – that things will become clear as we go onwards into the future. For now, we see through a glass, darkly. We do not know all, but we will know later. And meanwhile, we trust to love, to keep us close while we are waiting.

George Fox wrote to his parents in 1652:

Oh be faithful! Look not back, nor be too forward, further than ye have attained; for ye have no time but this present time: therefore, prize your time for your souls' sake. (Fox, 1831: epistle 5)

The wise son is advising his elders. To me, this sounds like Jesus admonishing his own parents after they discover him preaching in the Temple of Jerusalem (Luke 2:41–52). As Moltmann warns us, we need to hold on to hope. He quotes John Chrysostom: "It is not so much sin that plunges us into disaster, as rather despair" (Moltmann, 2014: 14). We live in an age of cynicism and pessimism.

But consider these words in Revelation 21:5: "I am making all things new" – remember that George Fox particularly liked the book of Revelation. Or recall the confidence of Hebrews 6:19:

> We have this hope, a sure and steadfast anchor of the soul, a hope that enters the inner shrine behind the curtain.

I remember speaking at a conference in Jerusalem about children with disabilities. In the question and answer session afterwards, an Orthodox couple told me about their son with a disability. They cherished him and had brought him up to feel good about himself. But when he attended school, he compared himself to the other children and felt downhearted. Everything was so much more difficult for him. Why did he have these problems? They asked me: "What can we say to our son?" and I was stuck. I did not know how to answer them. And then I remembered these words of the Talmud: "Every blade of grass has an angel bending over it saying grow, grow" (Midrash Rabba, Bereshit 10:6), and I told them to say that to their son. We are all worthy. We are each important. We grow. We don't have to catch up with anyone else. We can all grow in our own time, in our own way. But perhaps I should have reminded them of Psalm 139:14: "I praise you, because I am fearfully and wonderfully made." We are all made in the image of God.

So much of modern life is utilitarian arithmetic. We compete for success. We look for justice, for a fair return for our efforts. I do this, and therefore I deserve that. But God does not work like this at all. The message I take from what Jesus said in the New Testament is that our efforts are not entered into a ledger, like a profit-and-loss account. The repeated message of the Gospel is that it is not about our own efforts. I love the parable of the vineyard in Matthew 20. The workers start at dawn, or they start at nine, or they start at noon, or they start at three, or they start at five, and they all work until sundown. But then everyone who worked in the vineyard gets the same pay: one denarius, the daily wage. The workers who started at dawn are angry that they get no more than the workers who started in the afternoon. But the owner says, "Am I not allowed to do what I choose with what belongs to me? Or are you envious because I am generous?" Jesus adds, "So the last will be first, and the first will be last."

That is the topsy-turvy topology of the Kingdom of God (as my friend Sally Phillips describes it in her sermons, following another preacher, John Irvine). It is not about excelling more than others. It is not about just deserts. It is about love. The prodigal son is greeted with forgiveness, even though he does not deserve it, at least according to his brother. Think about Martha and Mary: it is the sister who neglects her chores to sit with Jesus who gets it right. Think about that costly alabaster box of perfume, which Judas feels could have been spent so much more wisely than anointing the feet of Jesus with it.

God is revealed through weakness not strength, through failure not success, through need not independence. We answer that of God in everyone, and we welcome everyone to the great feast – the poor, the crippled, the blind, and the lame – not the ones who were invited first. The criminal on the cross next to Jesus repents, acknowledges him and says: "Jesus, remember me when you come into your kingdom." That's a song worth singing, because Jesus replies to him, "Truly I tell you, today you will be with me in Paradise" (Luke 23:42–43).

We should look to the evidence for the building of the Kingdom of Heaven right here. I am not so bothered, frankly, with the life of the world to come. What will be, will be. The Kingdom of Heaven is a way of acting now, a way of being in this world. The Kingdom is about making a better today, not "pie in the sky when you die". The Kingdom, for Paul, meant the transformed human condition, a humanity free of selfishness, when the will of God and human desire are united (Dandelion et al., 1998). As the *Catechism of the Catholic Church* says:

> Already the final age of the world is with us and the renewal of the world is irrevocably under way. (Catholic Church, 1992: 670)

CHAPTER 3

You have no time but this present time

By the rivers of Babylon – there we sat down and there we wept when we remembered Zion. (Psalm 137:1)

One of my disability heroes, Antonio Gramsci, was an Italian communist intellectual, politically active during the 1920s and 1930s. A small, physically frail man, he was elected to the Italian parliament during the Fascist era, refused to escape to Moscow like his comrades, and under Mussolini was put in prison, where he ultimately died. At his trial, the prosecutor said, "We must stop this brain from working for 20 years" (Joll, 1977: 73), which is an epitaph of which any of us should be proud. But I want to remember Gramsci's famous motto, which was "Pessimism of the intellect, optimism of the will" (Gramsci, 1994: 299). Maybe it's apt to remember how people have survived equally bad or even worse times before, such as the era of the 1930s. So where and how could we be optimistic in 2020? Where is this spirit of resilience? What is there to sing about?

As Martin Luther King said the night before he was assassinated (like Moses, who gazed into the Promised Land but did not set foot in it himself), it may be that change is coming... but it may not be coming for us. It is remarkable that children and young people have been central to the climate strikes, led by that extraordinary young woman Greta Thunberg, a person with disability, who can see what her elders have failed to see and acted courageously when older people have failed to act. I am reminded of the children of a 17th-century Quaker meeting who kept the meeting for worship going when their parents were in prison. Jesus says repeatedly in the Gospels that young people can see what adults do not: more of that topsy-turvy described by Sally Phillips.

Getting the right perspective

Faced with grim news of climate change and conflict and division, I think we have to remember and have faith: things will not always be like this. A change is going to come (Solnit, 2016). As the poet Shelley reminds us in "Ozymandias", self-important tyrants are eventually toppled, sometimes literally, however much they say,

"Look on my works, ye mighty, and despair." As we look about us, we may find it difficult to perceive signs of hope. We may be filled with despair. But, and with apologies that this metaphor is not obvious for people with sight loss, I want to suggest different ways we might want to look. In the next sections I advocate the bigger picture, the close-up, the long view. I want to say: we may need to swap around our lenses from time to time, if we are to see everything clearly. If vision is not your thing, consider how you might listen differently. If neither sound nor vision is your thing, then it's about thinking differently. The message still applies. It is about the different stories that we need to tell, and the different perspectives we should take. I want to tell some stories about Britain today. Plus some others about the wider world drawn from my experiences with international development.

First, we might want to put things in perspective. In particular, I think humans are often very influenced by individual stories and do not always see the bigger picture. We tend to have 'headline anxiety'. Being bombarded by information every hour or every minute can feel like persecution. Maybe we need to be a bit more shallow sometimes. Worrying about stuff we can't affect is pointless – it is far better to let some of it wash over us.

Although I turn to calming Radio 3 more often these days, I particularly like the Radio 4 programme *More or less*, in which the economist Tim Harford takes a media story and analyses it, giving us the data and sometimes showing that the problem is less acute than it appears from the headlines. The late Swedish academic Hans Rosling referred to 'factfulness' as a means of keeping world news in perspective. He said he was not a naive optimist – he was a possibilist, meaning that he had a worldview that was constructive and useful. If we focus on the bigger picture, such as the proportion of people living in extreme poverty having halved in the past 20 years, it may be easier to remain hopeful. Rosling (2018) called it "understanding as a source of mental peace". He said: "When you hear about something terrible, calm yourself by asking: if there had been a positive improvement, would I have heard about that?"

We believe that the world is going to hell in a handcart, but that's simply not true. My cousin the *New York Times* journalist Nicholas Kristof (2019) reminds us:

> Every single day in recent years, another 325,000 people got their first access to electricity. Each day, more than 200,000 got piped water for the first time. And some 650,000 went online for the first time, every single day.

The statistics continue, taken from the World Bank and other reputable sources. Historically, nearly half of all children died before adulthood. In 1950, approximately one quarter died in childhood. Now less than 5 per cent do. Today, 10 per cent of people live in extreme poverty, defined as subsisting on less than $2 per day, but in 1981, 42 per cent of people lived in extreme poverty. Now, around 85 per cent of the world's population are literate; when I was born in 1966, the rate was less than half the population. According to the World Bank, in 1998, 381 million children were out of school; in 2014, this number had fallen to 263 million children, although the global population of children aged under 15 had grown from 1.85 to 1.92 billion (Rosling, 2018).

There are debates about other figures. For example, in his book *The better angels of our nature* (2011), Stephen Pinker maintains that global violence has fallen precipitately. Others disagree, considering that Pinker is not counting all forms of violence. Deaths from armed conflict and terrorism more than doubled from 2007 to 2017 (Institute for Health Metrics and Evaluation, 2018).

One question is about framing, by which I mean what is remembered and what is unheard, and how things are presented. The psychologists Daniel Kahneman and Amos Tversky (see Kahneman, 2011) have shown how important framing is in our understanding of how things are. For example, when the phrase 'gay marriage' shifted to become 'equal marriage', it seemed unarguable. Of course no one could oppose that!

Today, too often we hear more about what goes wrong than about what goes well. The media focuses on disasters and bad news stories. As newsreader Martyn Lewis (1993) once famously said, successes and victories are less newsworthy. He now chairs a magazine titled, appropriately, *Positive news*, which celebrates all the good news stories that it can find. Given that psychology tells us how much better our brains are at holding on to the negative than the positive, this active effort does seem worthwhile.

But there's a danger in this attempt to counter biases. We might end up sounding like Pollyanna, in the 1913 novel by Eleanor H. Porter. Pollyanna goes around playing 'The Glad Game', celebrating all the good news, until she loses the use of her legs. At this point, everyone rallies round and tells her how much she's meant to them. And soon after, she is miraculously cured. It's a bit like *It's a wonderful life*, only with Mary Pickford, not Jimmy Stewart. I think we should be very careful not to sound too much like plucky Pollyanna. We need to have a realistic view.

Alternatively, there is a school of thought, epitomised by writers such as Jonathan Haidt (2013), Bjorn Lomborg (2020), Steven Pinker (2019), and Matt Ridley (2010), that says we've got many of the bad things wrong anyway. Lomborg would tell us that global warming is real but not the end of the world, and we would be better off spending money on other things. Pinker wants to restore the Enlightenment faith in science, reason and humanism, thinks that most things are getting better for most people, and believes that inequality does not matter as much as we think. Haidt speaks up for the benefits of religion, not a fashionable topic these days. Ridley, a self-confessed 'rationalist optimist', places his hope in evolution and the free market, suggesting that we should not despair and should be ambitious.

While not rejecting everything these folk have to say, I do think we have to look disaster and potential disaster squarely in the face. All of these well-published prophets are on the conservative side of the scale. We should not pretend things are better than they are. In contrast, Nicholas Kristof (2019) is not a conservative, and I think his overall comments apply:

> I worry that deep pessimism about the state of the world is paralyzing rather than empowering; excessive pessimism can leave people feeling not just hopeless but also helpless.

Progress is possible, and this should not be a cause of complacency, but a spur to do more.

Framing remains very important. For example, the New Economics Foundation (2020) has worked hard to understand how people understand the British economy in its Framing the Economy research project. According to social research, Labour got it wrong in the 2019 UK general election by promoting a simple 'bash the rich' narrative. But the case for a better system can be made and won by focusing on the unfair manipulation of the system in the interests of the elites, and by talking instead about how a good society enables everyone to live a meaningful and fulfilling life. These are messages that speak to people.

Close up and personal

Second, we might want to look in close-up. What I mean is that if we take out our magnifying glass and look in detail, we may be able to observe examples of good practice that are obscure if we only glance, or rely solely on the national news. It's about exploring in microcosm – finding case studies of where good things are happening. We all know the proverb that says, "It is better to light a candle than to curse the darkness." Surely, George Fox would have been comfortable with that thought.

In last year's Swarthmore Lecture, Eden Grace (2019) told us positive stories of climate change resistance. Now I want to share some stories from Britain and overseas about young people, caregivers, homeless people, people with mental health issues, disabled people, and people with learning disabilities. These are often people at the margins, neglected in the rat race of profit and loss, seen as the failures that success inevitably leaves behind. But I think these are the people who Jesus was talking about in his parable of the great feast (Luke 14:15–24), not the rich and privileged and comfortable. As the Beatitudes (Matthew 5:3–12) confirm, the Gospels are about the excluded, not the comfortable.

For example, over the past few years, I have been doing research with **disabled people** in Africa who have had success. The story we get about disability in Africa is mostly negative. And it's true

– disabled kids are more likely to be out of school and households with disabled members face multi-dimensional poverty. There is a lot of ignorance and prejudice on the continent too. But this is not the whole story. Quite easily, my collaborators and I gathered more than 100 stories of disabled people in Kenya, Uganda and Zambia who had achieved success in their lives, on an equal basis to others (Shakespeare et al., 2019). They had demonstrated resilience, which is partly about their own determination and intelligence, but is also about the support they had received from family members who believed in them, teachers who had backed them, and organisations that had given concrete support, whether this consisted of giving them a wheelchair or paying their school or university fees. As a result, my respondents had ended up as civil servants or lawyers or farmers or teachers or shopkeepers: not necessarily wealthy but doing well, usually married and with kids of their own too, and helping others in their turn. For example, not only did these folk proudly tell me, "I was the only member of my family to finish school," but they were also supporting siblings, nephews or nieces through school, thereby 'paying it forward'. Every one of them challenges the stereotype that disabled people cannot succeed, that they are a bad investment, that they are not worth bothering with because they will never amount to anything. But none of them could have done it on their own.

Perhaps here I will be forgiven for sharing something more about myself. I was born with achondroplasia, which is more commonly known as dwarfism. I learned from my father, who also had the condition, not to feel exceptional. I went to boarding school and then to Cambridge. Blessed with a good brain and class privilege, I flourished. People stared and laughed at me, but I had good self-esteem and ignored them, as my father did. Throughout my twenties, my back problems got worse and I had more pain and restriction, but I still lived an ordinary life. At the age of 30, I suddenly developed very serious back problems, perhaps a disc prolapse, and I spent six months immobilised. That was a bad time, although I recovered almost completely. But after that, I had recurrent back problems and I was always fearful of a relapse of pain. In between episodes, life went on as usual. In fact, I was very fit: I cycled and danced and travelled.

In 2008, I was working in Geneva for the World Health Organization. I had had a bad summer of back pain – I realise now that I was overdoing things. Suddenly, over a day or two, I had a worsening of my back problem. First one leg, then the other became paralysed, and then I couldn't pass water. On 20 August, I flew home to Newcastle and checked myself into Newcastle General Hospital. The next morning, I had a decompression operation on my second lumbar vertebra. It didn't resolve the paralysis. I was now permanently unable to walk or move anything beneath my waist. After a struggle to get admission, I was transferred to the regional spinal injury unit at James Cook University Hospital in Middlesbrough. There I learned the tricks of the paraplegic trade. I also wrote sections of the *World report on disability* (World Health Organization, 2011) from my hospital bed. Seven weeks later I went home, unable to weight-bear, let alone walk. But I am proud to say that I returned to work at the World Health Organization in time for the International Day of Disabled Persons, on 3 December. Two years of outpatient physiotherapy followed, and I recovered a certain amount of strength and mobility.

I am not a hero, but I have certainly endured terrible pains and indignities. Lying in that hospital in Newcastle during those early weeks, I wanted to die. For the first time in my life, I was now dependent. Nurses did everything for me. But I rebuilt my life not because I am superhuman but because people adapt. You have no choice. You cope with restriction, and pain, and inconvenience, because you have no other option. Life goes on.

What to do? What everyone else does. People admire me, because they imagine how difficult life is. And it is sometimes difficult. But in the same situation, they would mostly do the same. There is always hope. Hope of getting on. Hope of finding joy, which I have certainly done and continue to do. As you would too. And that's the lesson of my story. There is always hope. People adapt. Life goes on. I remember saying at a research event that the worse thing I could ever imagine would be the death of one of my children. At a break, a colleague came up to me and said quietly, "My child died. It was terrible. But life goes on. You could survive even that."

Thinking of **people with intellectual disabilities**, who are often among the most marginalised, I want to mention two stories, one global and the other local (there are, of course, hundreds more). First, there is the story of the L'Arche movement (Vanier, 1999). This was initiated by the Canadian Jean Vanier in 1964. Vanier became aware of the thousands of people with intellectual disabilities who were institutionalised across France, and he invited two men to live with him in Trosly-Breuil, a place where he lived until he died on 7 May 2019. In 1968, the second L'Arche community was founded in Canada, as a home where non-disabled people live alongside people with intellectual disabilities in a spirit of equality and inclusion. There are now 147 communities in 35 countries around the world, including one in London. It started very small, but it was an inspirational idea that went viral, due to the commitment of people involved to a kind of justice that begins at home. Very disturbingly, at the time of writing this lecture (after Vanier's death), it was revealed that Vanier had sexually abused six women in France, none of whom had intellectual disabilities. While I utterly condemn this behaviour, which very sadly is not uncommon in religious contexts, I don't think that it undermines the values of L'Arche itself, which is bigger and more important than the failures of one individual.

People with intellectual disabilities do not want to be socially isolated, which they sometimes are in group homes set in the community but not of the community. Many of the people I spoke to in my research had experienced bullying. Before gathering these stories, I did not think it was possible that anyone could be so vile to people with intellectual disabilities. But I will never forget being told by someone of how they were taped to a tree in a park and urinated on. Almost every person with an intellectual disability has a similar story.

This is why WAVE for Change, an organisation based in Muswell Hill in London, is important. WAVE stands for 'We're All Valued Equally' and it is a social enterprise that aims to provide integrated spaces for those with learning disabilities and those without. WAVE runs a café, a weekly playgroup for families of children with special needs, a young adult group, an inclusive church, and much more than that, including extremely impressive research gauging attitudes to disability in its local area, and an award for the local business doing most to be inclusive of those with learning disabilities. WAVE stands for the unconditional love of God and the drive to build communities that are welcoming to all.

Disability is extremely diverse. I would include **people with mental health conditions** alongside other disabled people, and there are many examples from the UK and internationally of how community mobilisation can support people experiencing distress. In Norfolk, where I used to live, Sing Your Heart Out is a network of community singing workshops aimed at people who have had mental health problems (Shakespeare and Whieldon, 2018). But this is a voluntary arts group, not a branch of social services. People do not come as patients or professionals or members of the public. They come as individuals and there is no requirement to disclose anything about oneself. However, Sing Your Heart Out has become a lifeline to many people who have been receiving treatment for mental illness. As one participant said:

> It's given me a lot of confidence. I was scared and anxious and I was only used to unfriendly people. I got welcomed, the people were very nice. The coach gave me eye-contact and wanted to know my name and was considerate to me. She went out of her way, which is what she does for everybody. I really enjoyed it.

Each week, in four different towns across Norfolk, people gather for an afternoon of communal singing, with excellent singing teachers to guide them. The songs are familiar pop songs, folk songs and other simple music from around the world – there is now a Sing Your Heart Out songbook to draw on. However, there is no music to read or learn. The leader is there to guide people through the tunes by ear, and they soon become familiar.

Singing is powerful in itself, providing a sense of achieving a nice noise and making people feel part of something bigger than themselves. But the event is more than an arts project. The afternoon includes a tea break, with good biscuits, and there is conversation and sometimes problem-solving and referral to other sources of support. Importantly, this is all user-led activity:

> Gradually, as I got more and more drawn in and asked to do things, you feel you need to give more commitment and by giving more commitment you find you're more satisfied.

A regular Sing Your Heart Out event every week is sometimes the only activity for which people leave their homes. They are with friends, and they can relax and have refreshments and much-needed connection. People's morale improves, and they often even require less medication to calm and console them. Once a year, the four local workshops come together in an East Anglian town for the Big Sing, which often has well over 100 participants and is greatly enjoyed. This is a low-cost intervention, requiring only the room hire, refreshments and payment for the singing teachers.

Developed by Professor Dixon Chibanda (2017), the Friendship Bench intervention for common mental disorders has been running in Zimbabwe since 2006. After a successful trial, it has now been scaled up to more than 70 primary healthcare clinics in Zimbabwe. Lay health workers, most often grandmothers aged on average 58 with eight years of schooling, deliver a problem-solving intervention at a bench placed near a clinic. These ladies mainly previously worked in home-based care for people with HIV, care of people with tuberculosis, or community health education. There are now approximately 400 grandmothers involved as lay health workers, and about 30 grandfathers too.

There are usually six sessions lasting approximately 45 minutes each. The first session is problem identification, or opening the mind, *kuvhura pfungwa* in Shona. The client shares their story. Then comes problem exploration, or uplifting (*kusimudzira*). The health worker summarises what they have heard and helps the client to prioritise their problems and brainstorm solutions. The client comes up with specific, measurable, achievable, and realistic solutions. Next comes reassurance, or strengthening (*kusimbisa*), which involves checking to see whether all went well, making a home visit if necessary, and looking at obstacles and overcoming them.

After five sessions on the Friendship Bench, the client is invited to join a support group or circle (*kukatana tose*, which means 'holding hands together'). People get a chance to share their experiences, which are heard respectfully and confidentially. People are taught to crochet bags, baskets, mats, or purses from recycled plastic materials. This helps them to keep busy and productive, making their minds peaceful. The idea is that when one is crocheting, one cannot think too much (*kufungisisa*). The groups are there for a common purpose – mental health recovery and support – and this might involve singing or prayer.

The use of indigenous terms for distress, rather than stigmatised words such as 'mental illness' and 'counselling', means that the Friendship Bench intervention is more acceptable locally. WhatsApp and other mobile phone technologies ensure that communication can be maintained between the health workers and their supervisors, ensuring fidelity in the intervention. Grandmother Rudo says: "Friendship Bench has given me a sense of purpose in my community" (personal communication from Prof. Chibanda; see also www.friendshipbenchzimbabwe.org).

Quakers have always been greatly concerned about **violence and bullying**. Many will take heart from an intervention developed by my colleagues at the London School of Hygiene & Tropical Medicine called Learning Together, aimed at reducing bullying in schools. Bullying is more common among British young people than in other Western European countries. Cyber-bullying is very common. Any form of bullying can be both physically and mentally harmful, with effects that can be lifelong, including lower educational attainment.

Learning Together is an intervention based on a whole-school approach; it changes policies and systems, rather than just delivering lessons in class. A key element is to increase student engagement with school. The second important element is restorative justice, which aims to prevent or resolve conflicts between students, or between staff and students. When victims tell perpetrators how their behaviour has affected them, this can lead to a change in behaviour. People talk, and people listen, and reflection leads to improvements in future behaviour. The final element is social and emotional education, teaching young people the skills for managing emotions and relationships.

The Learning Together approach has been scientifically evaluated (Bonell et al., 2018). After the approach had been in place for two years, bullying had dropped by nearly 10 per cent. Students in the intervention schools had higher quality of life and wellbeing. They were also less likely to have tried alcohol or drugs or to be regular smokers. Moreover, this is a cheap intervention, as it simply relies on staff training to run the programme.

Another intervention, which helps to reduce gang violence, is the Unity Gym in Broomhall in Sheffield, established in 2010. This space offers mentoring and support to young people who are on the cusp of criminality or drifting into anti-social behaviour or involved in gangs. Some young people just need someone to talk to. Others want to train and work off steam: the gym's slogan is "transforming lives, one rep at a time," referring to the weights machines and other exercises that are repeated to develop strength and stamina. Unity Gym provides scope for healthy exercise, including basketball and other sports, at a time when there are fewer and fewer youth clubs and other services available to young people, especially during the school or college holidays.

Unity Gym (https://unitygym.org.uk) is about accepting everyone and seeing their potential, as well as listening to what they have to say about youth violence and knife crime. Inter-generational dialogue is vital, so that parents and older citizens understand the concerns of young people. Older folk mentor younger children: most of the work is done by volunteers. Unity Gym says, "we create positive spaces where differences are celebrated, knowledge is exchanged and talent is nurtured". Or, in less formal terms, the young people call it "the sanctuary of Broomhall" (Mason et al., n.d.).

Turning now to **homelessness**, there are many shelters operated by churches throughout the UK during the winter months. But on almost every Tuesday of the year, at a community kitchen in Ramsgate, the St George's Community Meal project brings together people who are homeless, have substance misuse problems or are simply isolated (Bailes, 2018). Folk might have had problems with Universal Credit, or homelessness, in a local economy (Thanet) that is far from resilient. But in fact, individuals don't have to fit into any 'vulnerable' category – they can just come along and be fed, and around 300 people turn up throughout the year, with about 40 people on a typical evening.

My colleague Maddy went along and said to me later:

> The thing I loved about it was that the focus was really on the friendship rather than the food... And the whole thing was just so unassuming. I actually thought it might have closed down when I arrived, because the building was in such a bad state. But inside, they were so very welcoming.

People arrive, get a name badge, eat some food, perhaps take part in a quiz, and above all chat. The project is staffed by volunteers from local churches and funded by the diocese. Local restaurants often help with providing the meals. Organiser Nigel Clarke says: "we have a real sense of community which is starting to build" (Bailes, 2018). And the project doesn't only operate on Tuesdays – volunteers spend the rest of the week linking people up to services or providing lifts or other support, for example, information about where to have a shower, get a meal or get clothes washed. It's a very low-key project, with a huge welcome for everyone.

What about **children in care**? New Beginnings is a project in Stockport run by Jadwiga Leigh, a former social worker and social work lecturer whom I interviewed for this book. She works with families who are known to local authority children's services. Often, these are mothers who are misusing alcohol or drugs, or who are survivors of domestic abuse, or mothers whose children have previously been removed by children's services. Once one child has been removed, commonly any future babies are removed too. So mothers are trapped and grieving in a cycle of misery and deprivation, their children raised in new homes far away, all at the expense of the state.

New Beginnings is inspired by the practice of Flemish professionals at Stobbe, which aims to work in partnership with families in the child protection process. Whereas Stobbe is a residential programme, New Beginnings is a community-based project. The key difference between New Beginnings and other parenting courses is that this project recognises that "parents are yesterday's children", as Leigh said when I interviewed her. Most 'failing' mothers are themselves victims of abuse, poverty and exclusion. Over 24 weeks, mothers are taken through a therapeutic process that helps them to recognise how historical and wider contextual issues have caused the problems they face today. This is very important: instead of labelling the parent as the problem, the problem is externalised, using a social–ecological approach. Mothers are supported with complementary therapies, arts and a lot of talking.

Whereas children's services might work with one family or one mother separately, isolating them from other families, New Beginnings enables mothers to connect with each other. They feel less alone. The narrative shifts for children's services as well as for the women as the social workers start to see the mothers make the changes they want to make. New Beginnings advocates and supports the women, using trust and relationships as its foundation: Leigh talks about "connection before correction". Whereas children's services expect parents to act as if they were professionals, Leigh, knowing the system from the inside, helps mothers to gain cultural capital – what she calls "the invisible rule book" – by showing them what they need to do in order to navigate the child protection system. At the time I spoke to her, 11 parents had completed the course. Ten were no longer being monitored by children's services, and some had no social care intervention whatsoever. Sometimes, children who had previously been removed had been returned to their families. Five of the women had gone through training and become peer mentors. Three peer mentors now actively work with the core team for the next set of parents who have joined the New Beginnings project. This further builds their sense of agency and capability.

Leigh is an inspirational leader, and New Beginnings would be nothing without her. That's why it's hard for other local authorities to replicate the model, even though they would clearly like to. They need to find other people like Leigh and empower them to grow grassroots projects in their own areas because the potential benefits are huge. Fostering and adoption are costly, difficult processes that are often second best for children. Investing in mothers, working with people rather than doing to people, offering therapy not punishment, enabling women to connect with each other (the power of the maternal commons): all have proven success in overcoming this social problem. New Beginnings gives hope for mothers who have previously felt stigmatised and isolated.

These are stories that you may never have heard, because we have an incomplete picture of our society. We don't see what is happening beneath the surface. The COVID-19 pandemic brought some of them to light, in the way that friends, and even strangers, helped each other. We usually hear of senseless tragedies, not signs of hope. These stories are central to my theme in this book, in multiple ways. First, they tell us that good things are happening, when we look close up. Second, these examples provide further evidence that human beings have the capacity to bounce back, to adapt, to be resilient, to make the best of things. And perhaps most importantly, they are evidence that when people work together for a common purpose, things improve. A change is going to come.

Many of these stories remind me of the five ways to wellbeing, which were developed by the New Economics Foundation and have been adopted by the NHS and many other agencies worldwide (Hey, 2017). The first is to connect with other people. The second is to be physically active. The third is to learn new skills. The fourth is to give to others. The fifth is to pay attention to the present moment. Probably all of these projects embody these five ways to wellbeing, which is important for beneficiaries, staff and volunteers alike in achieving positive mental health and inclusion. Another lesson is that most of this work is done by voluntary effort. If you believe in people, rather than resort to stereotypes, they can be different. They can fulfil your hopes for them. Disempowered and alienated people become less marginalised, more capable. The power is in their hands. Their families benefit. Society benefits. Things can change. Together we are building the Kingdom of Heaven.

Sub specie aeternitatis

Finally, we might like to take the long view. Bad things are hard (sometimes impossible) to endure, but everything passes. In Britain, the Blitz must have been terrifying. In my local park in Kennington, there is a very moving memorial to those who died when an air raid shelter – simply a network of trenches in the ground – had a direct hit from an aerial bomb. Mostly women and children, the youngest just three months old, were killed – at least 104 and maybe more (no final tally was ever made because bodies were torn apart). The memorial stone put up in 2006 has a quotation from Maya Angelou:

> History, despite its wrenching pain, cannot be unlived, but if faced with courage need not be lived again.

Across Britain, approximately 40,000 people died as a result of the wartime bombing. It is also important to remember that just in the fire-bombing of Dresden by the Allied Forces in February 1944, up to 25,000 people died. And I think that's what I mean by saying a long view helps. We mustn't forget, but we should move on. As with the terrible events of the Holocaust, we can never not remember. There are lessons to learn. But we do not have to live this terror every day.

For example, in our times, there is the story of HIV/AIDS. HIV was the big threat in the 1990s. My generation of young people were terrified of it. In the West, many thousands of gay men died, as did others, particularly those who were drug users or haemophiliacs, or had sex with men. There were many tragedies, and most of us lost friends. In Africa, millions died. Across the world, people with the virus became treatment activists, demanding better medical remedies. Others became prevention activists, promoting safe sex and community mobilisation. I remember, in Newcastle, working with the MESMAC project, which aims to strengthen the gay community and the wider community of men who have sex with men. I remember going around rowdy working-class pubs in Gateshead in the early 1990s, running a pub quiz about safe sex, with condoms and lube as prizes. Our theory was that talking about sex was the first stage to negotiating sex and not only having safe sex but also having better sex, for everyone, straight as well as gay. It was a big laugh about a huge issue, and a tiny part of the change that was needed.

Eventually, after a long struggle by treatment activists and hard work by researchers, combination therapies arrived. These prevent the virus causing havoc with health. Next there came the drug PrEP, which prevents transmission (and how proud we should be of Mags Portman, the great advocate of pre-exposure prophylaxis, who went to a Quaker school!). In the West, almost nobody dies of AIDS any more. In Africa, hundreds of thousands are still dying, and there are many orphans. An estimated 770,000 people died worldwide of AIDS in 2018, but that marks a 56 per cent reduction from 2004 (UNAIDS, 2019). One of my Ugandan colleagues lost six of his siblings to AIDS: only three of them are left. Many people I have spoken to or worked with in Africa are bringing up nephews or nieces or unrelated children, because their parents are 'late', in other words dead. But even in Africa, the worst of the epidemic seems to have passed. We have all seen films and read books on the topic of AIDS, but I hope we never forget the heroism and solidarity of the people who endured the epidemic, or who died in it, or who loved those who died. A staggering 32 million people have died worldwide as a result of HIV (UNAIDS, 2019). While a greater number than that are currently infected with the virus, due to drug therapies almost all of them will lead longer lives than they would have in the past, and there are also fewer new infections because the virus is suppressed in those on treatment.

It's not just that bad things end and time passes. *Sub specie aeternitatis* is 17th-century philosopher Baruch Spinoza's phrase for putting things into the context of eternity. It's a good exercise, particularly if you think you are very important, or if you think that someone else is pretty worthless or you think that a certain problem is irresolvable. If we take a long view, what does it matter what we have earned, or how many mountains we have climbed? Why does it matter that someone has intellectual disabilities? As an Italian proverb states, "After the game, the king and the pawn go into the same box." Another philosopher, Thomas Nagel (2008: 143) says that if we look at human life in this way, the view is "at once sobering and comical".

We usually take a subjective view, considering how things matter to us, whereas if we take an objective view, we might be more sanguine. I think that if we look from this long perspective, we can see that everything has a time under the heavens and that no American president, for example, can serve more than two terms. The Biblical tyrant Herod was eventually overthrown and eaten by worms. Millions were killed in the Civil War, in the Holocaust, in Mao's forced collectivisation. But we can see that disasters give way to recovery, that problems can be mitigated, that good triumphs in the end.

I am not saying that all those deaths did not matter in the long run. I do not want anyone to be complacent at all, although from time to time we might want to respond with the ironic smile that Thomas Nagel (2008) recommends. Usually, things rally because of human collective action – as with the school climate strikes, Extinction Rebellion and HIV treatment activism – which shows that we should not simply surrender to events that we believe we cannot control. But if we take a long view, then we might be less pessimistic about everyday problems and more hopeful about long-term resolutions. In the poem "Everyone Sang" by Siegfried Sassoon, there are tears and horror, but "the singing will never be done".

CHAPTER 4

Optimism of the will

In chapter 3, I quoted the motto that Antonio Gramsci (1994: 299) repeated during his many years in prison: "Pessimism of the intellect, optimism of the will." This is not just a hopeful couplet to console us while we wait for things to improve. It is an injunction to action. It is not the anonymous forces of history that bring down the dictator, it is collective human action. It may be the cumulative effect of small acts of protest leading to small changes, or large ones like Extinction Rebellion and the Stansted 15, who blocked a deportation flight. It may be the threat of the good example. We are for justice and mercy and truth and peace and true freedom, that these may be exalted in our nation.

While I was writing this book, I went to Sri Lanka for a week. I had been working in Tamil Nadu (India) and I was due to go to Dhaka (Bangladesh) next for more work, and it was the easiest thing to hop over to Colombo in the meantime. I felt combining three activities in one long-haul return flight was more justifiable, given the climate emergency. There is a sense in which going to Sri Lanka feels like going home, even though I have never lived there. It's where my mother's family come from. She was born in Colombo, and her parents were born in Kandy, the town in the hills that was once the capital of the Sinhala kingdom of Ceylon. Her ancestors came from Europe as lawyers or engineers or minor colonial administrators; they married Sinhala women and lived the life described in Michael Ondaatje's lovely memoir *Running in the family* (1982). There are many reasons to praise Sri Lanka: it's a beautiful island, it has a cuisine that I would rank better than any, and it's a great place to see leopards and elephants and birds and bears. But above all, the people are ingenious and creative and if it were not for a grim history of strife and mismanagement, it would now be one of the superpowers of Asia.

Things don't always go right in Sri Lanka, any more than in the rest of the world. But what I particularly appreciate is the ubiquitous Sri Lankan response to difficulty and disaster. When the railway breaks down, or the shower fails, or the flight is cancelled, the Sri Lankan replies with the deathless phrase, "What to do?" This does not mean, "What shall we do?" It is not a request for help. It is an admission that the situation is helpless. "What to do?" literally means "What can be done?" or "It can't be helped," according to Michael Meyler's excellent *Dictionary of Sri Lankan English* (2007). But as used in that island (and by me in these islands), it means more than that.

"What to do?" means "What did you expect?" and "This is what life is like" and "This is the sort of thing that happens." It communicates a sense of fatalism and acceptance. In Manuka Wijesinghe's *Monsoons and potholes* (2006: 16), a character calls it "the poor man's karma". The phrase reminds me of something they often say in Vienna. An Austrian emperor is said to have contrasted Berlin, where things were "serious but not hopeless", with Vienna, where "the situation is hopeless, but not serious". I think I know which of the two I prefer.

"What to do?" suggests that there are some things that one just has to put up with. There is no use fighting everything. Some fates just have to be endured, like Job with his boils. To Jews, Christians and Muslims, Job is the archetypal figure who remains steadfast, despite his suffering, despite not knowing why bad things are happening to him. And in the end, for Job at least, everything turns out well.

Sometimes, over-thinking is the worst response. Sometimes, fighting is the worst response. Acceptance helps. Distraction is good. For example, when we are enduring chronic pain, not focusing on the problem is best. Evidence shows that when people with chronic pain have solicitous partners, they report worse pain. In other words, if someone is always asking you about your pain, then you will focus on your pain and feel it more acutely. If everyone ignores it, and you find distractions, then the pain will be less present and thus less of a problem. I am not suggesting simple 'mind over matter'. The pain is real and does not go away. But the more you concentrate on it, the worse it gets.

I feel that what is true of physical pain may be true of many problems and difficulties in life. Often, we seek to control things by understanding them. We think that if we see what caused them, we might be able to solve them, or at least prevent them recurring. Yet many difficulties either cannot be understood or else cannot be prevented. In these cases, maybe, we just have to find ways to endure. It's an exercise in understanding our limitations. Disasters happen. Medicine fails us. Not everything can be fixed. Contrary to what that Austrian emperor said, helpless does not mean hopeless, and resignation is not the same as despair. Hope is a necessary approach for everyone, a buttress against despair. For Søren Kierkegaard (1989), despair, the "sickness unto death", is necessary for us truly to have hope in God, to allow the life of the spirit to break through from the ground up. And we should always have hope.

Philosophers define hope as a desire for a state of affairs coupled with the belief that it is possible, even if not certain. We don't bother hoping for something that we are certain we are going to get. Nor do we hope for something that we know we will not get. Remember Paul. In palliative care, when a person is suffering from terminal illness, caregivers have to be careful not to promote false hope, which would be dishonest and misleading, even if it improved the wellbeing of the individual. Benevolent paternalism is no longer the acceptable approach for healthcare workers. At the same time, for a patient to lose all hope would be very bad for their wellbeing.

Hope is different from optimism, which is a general disposition to think things will get better; this is because hope usually has a specific focus. A rational hope has a higher chance of fulfilment; an irrational hope is based on a false or over-optimistic belief. In illness, hope is very helpful, in improving wellbeing and avoiding depression. Hope also predicts the extent to which patients will follow medical advice (Legg et al., 2015). Yet to think in terms of miracle cures or to over-inflate the chances that a treatment will be successful would be unrealistic or dishonest. It would be a deception that undermines patient autonomy.

Gabriel Marcel gives us a way through this dilemma by talking about the experience of hope, particularly hope against hope (see Garrard and Wrigley, 2009; Webb, 2007). He talks about "absolute hope" rather than hope for something specific, based on his thoughts about prisoners in World War I and the danger of despair. For Marcel, despair entails a) capitulation to your fate; b) the idea that time is closed and will bring no positive change; and c) turning inward and away from others. Conversely, absolute hope means a) maintaining a sense of self, sometimes called "living until you die"; b) waiting patiently and actively, not fixating on the inevitable end, and being open to new experiences; and c) maintaining a communal aspect to life or having hope in someone. This distinction leads to hopefulness rather than false hope. Absolute hope prevents the descent into despair, but it is not based on an illusion or false optimism. It just does not allow the negative information to saturate all other aspects of life.

In the Bible, there is a virtue that is rarely mentioned today: fortitude, which means firmness in difficulties. Aristotle (1980: 40) talks about having an appropriate balance of fear and confidence in relation to courage. Thomas Aquinas (2018: 6) talks about "brave endurance" and rates fortitude among the cardinal virtues. I don't think you have to be a theist to consider these important virtues. Psychologists might prefer to talk in terms of resilience. It's important to highlight that it does not take a special person to be courageous or resilient. We should not think that some people are heroic and other people are not. There is a danger in thinking we are inadequate compared to 'heroes'. The virtue of resilience is an ordinary magic, to use Ann Masten's (2014) phrase, which all human beings possess. Faced by adversity, the common response is to cope, adapt and survive.

In a world preoccupied by climate catastrophe, pandemic disease, poverty, and a threatened economic downturn, saying "What to do?" does not mean we simply throw up our hands and give up. It is not the same fatalism as concluding "It is the will of God" and that therefore there is nothing to be done. Quakers are working for the Kingdom of God today. We have hope. We know we can make a difference. "What to do?" is completely compatible with working patiently and with others to improve our society and restore our environment. As Grace Paley says, "The only recognizable feature of hope is action" (Legg et al., 2015: 3034). So Samuel Beckett (1986: 90), in *Worstward Ho*, writes: "No choice but stand. Somehow up and stand. Somehow stand."

We need to strike a balance between taking action and not feeling we have to do everything ourselves. Jürgen Moltmann, in his 1967 book *Theology of hope*, distinguishes between the hopelessness of Prometheus (which is about going beyond your guide, not waiting in patience) versus the hopelessness of Sisyphus (no point in doing anything, the relentlessness of effort). While it is better to light a candle than to curse the darkness, we also need to remember that each of us is only one flame among the many. But as the philosopher John Locke (1824: 34), wrote, "The candle that is set up in us shines bright enough for all our purposes."

I believe that human decency is a benign acid that corrodes evil everywhere and that demonstrates the value of resistance and solidarity, and I think we do well to remember that. In January 2019, I visited Yad Vashem, the Holocaust exhibition in Jerusalem. Among indescribable suffering and barbarity, it was the stories of the 'Righteous Among the Nations' – people like Oskar Schindler, Irena Sendler, Hendrika Gerritsen, and other individuals who resisted the Nazi project – that filled me with hope, even when their personal actions were defeated. Remember, so far over 27,000 individuals (from 51 countries) have been recognised as among the Righteous Among the Nations. Read their stories, which I found easily on Wikipedia. In 2020, I was lucky enough to meet the film maker Agnieszka Holland, whose own mother was one of the Righteous Among the Nations, having fought in the Warsaw Uprising.

The lesson I take from that resistance to the Holocaust is that we cannot be passive. Better days do not drop into our laps – they have to be actively worked for. This means taking responsibility, exercising agency and being grown up rather than resorting to the politics of victimhood and complaint. Depending on where and when we happen to live, sometimes it means being very brave indeed.

A Quaker ancestor, Mary Dyer, protested against harsh anti-Quaker laws in the new colony of Massachusetts. She bravely returned to Boston, defied those laws and was hanged for it. We might think of her martyrdom as stubborn and pointless, a waste of a life. Yet her execution led to Charles II writing to all the New England colonies a year later, thanks to the intercession of another Quaker, Edward Burrough, to tell them not to persecute Quakers and not to execute people for their beliefs. If we do genuinely follow the promptings of love and truth in our hearts, everything we do is worthwhile – even if the world does not think so. Trust that the leadings of love and truth will come right. Mary Dyer couldn't have done anything other than what she did.

Even under fascism, people resist, through similar extraordinary bravery. Hans Fallada's novel *Alone in Berlin*, originally published in 1948, is based on the true story of Otto and Elise Hampel, who distributed messages critical of the Nazi regime, and who were eventually located, and executed (Fallada, 2009). In another example, the White Rose student network protested in Munich, and Hans and Sophie Scholl and Christoph Probst were captured and executed by guillotine on 22 February 1943. Terrence Malick's film *A hidden life* (2019) offers the story of Franz Jägerstätter, who also resisted and died: he says, "I have this feeling inside me and I can't do what I believe is wrong. I want to save my life, but not through lies."

In the civil rights era, Rosa Parks refused to go to the back of the bus, where the black folk were meant to go. She resisted an unjust law. Men and women were whipped and clubbed in the Selma march and many other demonstrations, but they peacefully resisted. In South Africa, thousands burned their pass cards, Steve Biko was killed, Ruth First was blown up, Albie Sachs was maimed, Nelson Mandela was imprisoned, hundreds of others died. And still they resisted. Eventually, the Nazis were defeated, civil rights came to America and Apartheid was ended. Yet the struggle continues because the full promise of such victories is rarely achieved. And so we keep repeating 'Black Lives Matter' and the other slogans and movements of our own time.

At other times and for many of us, this mainly means small acts of resistance, which cost us comparatively little. They are not substitutes for the big actions, but they are part of the same story. The people who voluntarily agree to take fewer flights, to eat less meat and to contribute to foodbanks may not be solving the problems we face, but they are doing their bit too. I think it's a matter of inner, outer and across. Inner might mean changing your own lifestyle; outer might mean working for change in the world; across might mean making connections with other people, which will make both the inner and the outer work more likely to succeed. So Marilynne Robinson writes: "To value one another is our greatest safety, and to indulge in fear and contempt is our gravest error" (Robinson, 2015: 29).

Joanna Macy and Chris Johnstone (2012) talk about "active hope", which for them is a practice with three phases. First, we need a clear view of reality. Second, we need to identify what we are hoping for, so we know which direction to go in. Third, we need to take steps to move in that direction. We don't even need to feel optimistic – we just have to have an intention to act, a willingness to play a part in the transformation. Rather than either the "business as usual" narrative, in which nothing needs to change, or the "great unravelling" narrative, in which we're going to hell in a handcart, they offer the story of the "great turning", where we find and offer our gift of active hope, and develop new life-sustaining systems and practices. Optimists think everything will be fine without us doing anything – pessimists think that there's nothing we can do. But we should hold onto the certainty that what we do matters, although we cannot know the outcome, and it might even come long after our deaths, as Rebecca Solnit (2016) reminds us.

This is where we should put our energy, just as the slavery abolitionists did, just as the League of Nations pioneers did, just as the civil rights marchers did, just as the Campaign for Nuclear Disarmament did in the 1950s and the 1980s, just as those struggling against Apartheid did. Remembering that collective action and the work of truth and justice have generated victories is very important. As Charles Dickens famously wrote at the start of *A tale of two cities* (1859): "It was the best of times; it was the worst of times." We cannot think that everything has always been grim and thankless, otherwise we would truly despair. Enthusiasm is a "valuable renewable resource" (Macy and Johnstone, 2012: 214). The work is difficult, but it is worthwhile. Richard Rohr says:

> Hope cannot be had by the individual if everything is corporately hopeless. It is hard to heal individuals when the whole thing is seen as unhealable. (Rohr, 2019: 46)

Rowan Williams (2012: 36) says we must be "able to withstand the pressures of a functionalist and reductionist climate". We need to challenge the dominant instrumentalism, to say that things and people and relationships and places are important in themselves, not just as means to an end. We need to challenge individualism and the pursuit of individual greed, which mean that the things we have in common, the global commons, are threatened. As Williams (2012: 177) says, responding appropriately to creation is part of responding appropriately to God.

We need to be clear about what results from the impact of our individual lives and what is the consequence of wider structures. I think we can work on both:

- We need to change lifestyles: I think of this as our inner work.
- We need to work for change: I think of this as our outer work.
- To make both succeed, we need to make connections: I think of this as us working across barriers. We are all interdependent. We do better with others.

Inner, outer and across. We have to have all three, to fully realise the potential that each of us has, to make the difference that we can make together, and to do it as one. Doing good on our doorsteps or in our kitchens is not enough unless we help make public good break out in the world. And we cannot make that happen unless we link up with others, regardless of who they are and what they bring. Almost nobody can do it alone. Inner, outer and across.

As Samuel Beckett (1986: 90) urges us in *Worstward Ho*, "Fail again. Fail better." We might improve things if we listened better, but we will still not always succeed. That's also the message of Penelope Fitzgerald's rather bleak little book *The bookshop* (1978). It is human to fail. The prophets in the Bible were none of them optimists; they preached doom much of the time, but they had a hopeful message from God.

Some of us suffer – in fact, I would say that most of us suffer in some ways and at some time. But as Kierkegaard wrote, suffering is not a good, any more than despair is (Kierkegaard, 1989). We should not wallow in it, and suffering does not make us pure or good. Suffering is given to us to be striven against, not embraced. Hugh Pyper (2011: 8) writes: "The possibility of blessedness is only available to us because we are constituted to despair." Joy is a command from God. As Kierkegaard also wrote: "The religious person is one who has discovered the comic on the greatest scale" (Kierkegaard, 2009: 462). Or as it says in 1 Corinthians 3:18, "If you think that you are wise in this age, you should become fools so that you may become wise." More topsy-turvy topology of the Kingdom of God.

To ask "Where is the hope?" is to ask where is the cause that can inspire – not just us, but the whole world; where we can bear witness; where we can make a difference; where we can change things. The answers will be different for each of us. But we should hold on to the fact that we can definitely make a difference, small or large. Our Friend Eden Grace, giving the 2019 Swarthmore Lecture, concluded her text by asking us "to say yes to the power and love of the ocean, to be propelled onward as an instrument of the Ocean of Light that is already, right now, transforming the world" (Grace, 2019: 111).

We are for justice and mercy and truth and peace and true freedom, that these may be exalted in our nation. Remember Archimedes, the Greek engineer and thinker, who said that he could move the world if had "a lever and a place to stand". So, what is our lever? Our lever is love. And where must we stand? Where we find ourselves. Where we sit and stand right now, as we hear this and as we read this. That is our lever. Here is our place to stand.

In these efforts, we should expect setbacks, and we should not be hard on ourselves, let alone anyone else. We are all flawed human beings. Immanuel Kant (1991: 46) said, "Nothing straight can be constructed from such warped wood as that which man is made of." As Quakers, we do not think we are perfect – but we think we can be perfected. We are constantly striving, even though, like Moses, we never quite make it. And the Bible is full of precedents for this. The prophets endured defeat, exile and the destruction of their Temple. Søren Kierkegaard remarked that the Hebrew Bible can be summed up in the word "nevertheless" (Pyper, 2011: 6). And remember Hillel, who was born into Babylonian exile but died in Jerusalem – Hillel, who is renowned for his commitment to the repair of the world:

> If I am not for myself, who will be for me? But if I am only for myself, who am I? If not now, when? (Pirkei Avot 1:14)

REFLECTING ON AND ENGAGING WITH THE LECTURE

The following questions are designed to help Friends to look at this Swarthmore Lecture, to reflect on our own experience of and understanding of hope. They can be used by individuals or for group work.

Using these questions

These questions can be used very flexibly and with minimal or no equipment. Participants may wish to bring pens and paper or notebooks for their own notes.

There are a large number of questions and the intention is that these could be used over a number of sessions or the group could pick and choose which questions it wants to focus on, going at a pace that suits the group. We recommend that each session runs for a maximum of 90 minutes.

Guidance for facilitators and group members

In undertaking exploration of the themes of the lecture it is important that all participants come with heart and mind prepared. It is probably helpful for some members of each group to be designated as 'facilitators', perhaps on a rotating basis, to guide the group through the process, keep an eye on time and 'hold' the group. It may be appropriate for them to decide the order in which the group approaches the questions, the methods used and the framework in which the group will work. Everyone else should not come expecting to be directed or merely guided through the process but should engage fully and wholeheartedly. As Friends, we do not have a separated priesthood, and all have the clergy's responsibility for the maintenance of the meeting as a community. Similarly, in our groups, we all hold the responsibility to work collaboratively in order for the group to work together, enabling us to reflect on our spiritual journeys and helping us to see the Light in our lives, and in the community in which we worship together.

Discuss and agree how the group will work together

In small groups and whole meeting groups, all members of the group should have a chance to share, and one or two persons should not dominate the spoken contributions (this includes the facilitators). It may be helpful to state a few general guidelines, which are the foundation for the approaches below:

- **Come to the group with as much of ourselves as possible.** This means two things: to be as present as we can be (which may differ depending on the day, or the time of day or what else is happening) and to bring all of who we are – our joys and successes, our fears and failings. You may pass if you do not wish to speak to the topic or answer a question.
- **Presume welcome and extend welcome.** We support each other's participation and growth by giving and receiving hospitality.
- **No fixing**. No fixing, counselling or setting straight. Facilitators and fellow participants should support each other rather than try to set each other straight.
- **When the going gets tough, turn to wonder.** When you find yourself reacting harshly, disagreeing with another, becoming judgemental or becoming defensive, ask questions such as, "I wonder what my reaction teaches me about myself."
- **Speak for self.** Using 'I' statements, speak your truth in a way that respects the truths of others. Speak for a second time only after others have had a chance to speak once.
- **Listen with 'soft eyes'.** Listen to others with eyes of compassion and understanding.
- **Trust and learn from silence.** Silence is a rare gift in our busy world. Allow silence to be another member of the group. Leave silence between speakers.
- **Observe confidentiality.** The main issue in relation to confidentiality is how agreeing exceptions will work in practice.

There will be times when people share ideas, approaches or experiences that are helpful to others. It is part of our Quaker tradition that we share and learn from each other within the priesthood of all believers. However, it is important to respect individuals' personal stories. A general principle is that it is okay to share ideas but not personal stories. The following is a suggestion that you can adapt to suit your group:

– Everything shared in pairs and small groups is confidential to those present *except for* agreed things, which may be reported to the main group and discussed during the session.
– Everything shared in the whole group stays in the group and is not discussed outside the session *except for* agreed things, which may be discussed outside the session between course members only.

• **Accept imperfection**. In ourselves and in others.

Approaches for group work[1]

Creative listening
Participants take turns around the circle, giving each person a chance to say something on the topic. Limiting the responses to two or three minutes may be useful so that the entire time is not used in this one go-round.

• Each offering is given without expectation of questions or comments from others in the group.
• To help share time equally, a watch may be held by the person who has just spoken and handed to the next speaker at the end of the allotted time.

Creative listening may also be used for longer contributions, in which case people may contribute in any order. Two suggestions to encourage equal participation are:

• **Talking stick.** An object, such as a shell, smooth pebble or pine

1 Adapted with permission from *Hearts & minds prepared facilitator handbook*, published by Woodbrooke Quaker Study Centre, 2003.

cone, is picked up by a speaker, who must not be interrupted while holding it. The object can be picked up by anyone for their turn after it has been replaced in the centre of the circle. Some Native North American groups call it the 'talking stick'. This method is usually most effective when linked with periods of silent worship in between contributions.

- **Stones or tokens**. Try giving two or three stones or other small objects to each person, each 'worth' two minutes. After a minute or so at the start, anyone may toss one into the middle of the circle to signify that they are ready to use the next two minutes of the group's time. A timekeeper can be used. As in the 'go-round', no comments or questions should be allowed to follow the offerings.

Worship sharing

This can be particularly suitable for potentially controversial, difficult or personal topics. It differs from creative listening in that it is based less on thinking than on surrendering ourselves to worship and accepting what emerges. Although participants are asked to reflect on the questions in advance, contributions are likely to be at a deeper level, sometimes surprising to the speakers themselves. Here, it is usually best to state the question or issue, and then start with a short period of silence (about five minutes) in which each person moves into worship and thinks of the contribution they may feel called to make. People then speak in any order. Close with a period of silent worship.

- The emphasis is on worshipful listening.
- The group may agree before starting to place time limitations on each person so that everyone has a chance to speak. In this case, if one person is approaching the time limit, the facilitator should intervene to ask that the speaker come to a conclusion.
- An object may be used as a talking stick if the group would find it helpful.

Working in pairs or small groups of 3–4

Pairs or small groups give each person time to speak in depth. These reflections need not be reported back to the whole group.

- The listener should not speak, though non-verbal signs of attention are helpful.
- It is fine for the speaker to be silent for a while if they want.
- The listener should be reminded not to respond to the first speaker when it is their turn to speak.

Group discussion

There may be times (especially in the activities of groups) when the give and take of a discussion can be appropriate – for example, when a full flow of ideas is wanted – and this might encourage some Friends to venture making contributions they were cautious of offering in other modes. It will be particularly important to encourage the quiet or reticent and not to let one or two Friends dominate the group.

In discussion, the facilitator has three main aims:

- to enable all to participate, not just the articulate and long-winded
- to keep the discussion to the point
- to prevent heated feelings from turning the discussion into an argument.

It is quite appropriate for the facilitator to ask for a minute or two of silence at any point if he or she feels this will help the group. You can also suggest that the group moves into creative listening mode so that the range of views can be heard without interruption.

Quick think

Ideas are produced rapidly (but perhaps giving someone enough time to record them) without further discussion or questioning. This is useful for bringing up a lot of suggestions that can then be used as material for a more reflective discussion.

READING GROUP SUGGESTIONS
FOR DISCUSSION

Introduction: Why are we hopeless?

- Why are we hopeless?
- What makes you feel hopeless today?
- How does the COVID-19 pandemic make you feel hopeless? How does it make you feel hopeful?
- Where do you find your hope?
- How would you support a F/friend who was feeling hopeless about contemporary society or politics?
- Choose one poem or song that gives you hope. How does it make you feel hopeful?

Chapter 1: Let your life preach

- What would George Fox or Isaac Penington have thought about the contemporary Religious Society of Friends?
- What would they have said to the current political leader of your country?
- What might they have done about climate change?
- How does this tradition impact you and your choices and actions today?
- How do the Quaker testimonies of peace, equality, truth, and simplicity relate to hope?
- Does meeting for worship contribute to feelings of hope?
- Should Quakers today really make themselves unpopular? How should they go about this? Whom should they be unpopular with?

Chapter 2: Faith, hope and love

- What stories or verses in the Gospels give you strength or make you feel hopeful?

- This Swarthmore Lecture suggests that Quakers are mystics. Do you think this is right?
- What does it mean to be a mystic today?
- What can Quakers learn from other faith communities about hope?
- How might you go about learning this?
- What have Quakers got that they can share with other faith communities about hope?
- How could you share?

Chapter 3: You have no time but this present time

- Does it help you to put the current situation in a different perspective?
- Could it be dangerous to do so?
- Which hopeful initiatives would you add to those discussed?
- What work comes easiest?
- What work is hardest?
- Are some initiatives more effective than others in inculcating hope?

Chapter 4: Optimism of the will

- Does past history make you more or less hopeful?
- Do you draw any lessons from history?
- Where could you find hope in a crisis such as the COVID-19 pandemic?
- Can you think of steps you need to take in your life, community and society to find hope? Does it help to group them into the categories of 'inner', 'outer' and 'across'?
- How does each relate to the other approaches?
- How much can you achieve on your own? How much requires others?
- Do you focus on one approach more than others? Why?
- What is your lever? Where is your place to stand?

BIBLIOGRAPHY

Aquinas, Thomas (2018). *Summa theologiae: Third part of the second part.* Woodstock, ON: Devoted Publishing.

Aristotle (1980). *Nichomachean ethics.* Oxford: Oxford University Press.

Bailes, Kathy (2018). 'Community meal project in Ramsgate helps hundreds of people who are homeless or isolated' in *The Isle of Thanet News*, 20 November, https://theisleofthanetnews.com/2018/11/20/community-meal-project-in-ramsgate-helps-hundreds-of-people-who-are-homeless-or-isolated, accessed 18 March 2020.

Beckett, Samuel (1986). *The complete dramatic works.* London: Faber.

Bonell, Chris, Elizabeth Allen, Emily Warren et al. (2018) 'Effects of the Learning Together intervention on bullying and aggression in English secondary schools (INCLUSIVE): A cluster randomised controlled trial' in *The Lancet*, vol. 392, 2452–2464.

Britain Yearly Meeting (2009). *Quaker faith & practice.* Fourth ed. London: Yearly Meeting of the Religious Society of Friends (Quakers) in Britain.

Butcher, Carmen Acevedo, trans. (2009). *The cloud of unknowing.* Boulder, CO: Shambhala Publications.

Catholic Church (1992). *Catechism of the Catholic Church.* Vatican City: Libreria Editrice Vaticana.

Chaplin, Jonathan (2008). *Talking God: The legitimacy of religious public reasoning.* London: Theos.

Chibanda, Dixon (2017). 'Reducing the treatment gap for mental, neurological and substance use disorders in Africa: lessons from the Friendship Bench' in *Epidemiology and psychiatric sciences*, vol. 26, 342–347.

Dandelion, Ben Pink (2014). *Open for transformation: Being Quaker.* London: Quaker Books.

Dandelion, Ben Pink, Douglas Gwyn and Timothy Peat (1998). *Heaven on earth: Quakers and the Second Coming.* Birmingham: Curlew Productions and Woodbrooke College.

Fallada, Hans (2009). *Alone in Berlin*. London: Penguin.

Fitzgerald, Penelope (1978). *The bookshop*. London: Duckworth.

Fox, George (1831). *A collection of many select and Christian epistles, letters and testimonies written on sundry occasions, by that ancient, eminent, faithful Friend, and minister of Christ Jesus, George Fox*. Philadelphia: Marcus T. C. Gould.

Fox, George (1952). *Journal*. Cambridge: Cambridge University Press.

Garrard, Eve and Anthony Wrigley (2009). 'Hope and terminal illness: False hope versus absolute hope' in *Clinical ethics*, 4, 38–43.

Giles, Chris (2019) 'The shifting patterns of UK inequality' in *Financial Times*, 14 May, https://www.ft.com/content/d70f351c-764d-11e9-bbad-7c18c0ea0201, accessed 11 March 2020.

Grace, Eden (2019). *On earth as it is in heaven: The Kingdom of God and the yearning of creation*. London: Quaker Books.

Gramsci, Antonio (1994). *Letters from prison*, volume 1, edited by Frank Rosengarten, translated by Raymond Rosenthal. New York: Columbia University Press.

Haidt, Jonathan (2013). *The righteous mind: How good people are divided by politics and religion*. London: Penguin.

Hampton, Jennifer May (2014). 'British Quaker survey: Examining religious beliefs and practices in the twenty-first century' in *Quaker studies*, 19, 7–136.

Hewitson, Gerald (2013). *Journey into life: Inheriting the story of early Friends*. London: Quaker Books.

Hey, Nancy (2017). 'Five ways to wellbeing in the UK' in *What works wellbeing*, 18 January, https://whatworkswellbeing.org/blog/five-ways-to-wellbeing-in-the-uk, accessed 24 March 2020.

Institute for Health Metrics and Evaluation (2018). *Findings from the Global Burden of Disease Study 2017*. Seattle: Institute for Health Metrics and Evaluation.

Joll, James (1977). *Gramsci*. Glasgow: Fontana Paperbacks.

Julian of Norwich (1980). *Revelations of divine love*, translated by James Walsh. Wheathamstead: Anthony Clarke Books.

Kahneman, Daniel (2011). *Thinking fast and slow*. New York: Farrar, Straus and Giroux.

Kant, Immanuel (1991). *Political writings*, edited by Hans Reiss, translated by H. B. Nisbet. Cambridge: Cambridge University Press.

Kierkegaard, Søren (1989). *The sickness unto death*, translated by Anthony Hannay. Harmondsworth: Penguin.

Kierkegaard, Søren (2009). *Concluding unscientific postscript*, translated by Anthony Hannay. Cambridge: Cambridge University Press.

King, Martin Luther (1962) 'Draft of Chapter X, "Shattered dreams"', https://kinginstitute.stanford.edu/king-papers//documents/draft-chapter-x-shattered-dreams, accessed 17 March 2020.

King, Martin Luther (1963). 'I have a dream', https://kinginstitute.stanford.edu/king-papers//documents/i-have-a-dream-address-delivered-march-washington-jobs-and-freedom, accessed 17 March 2020.

Kristof, Nicholas (2019). 'This has been the best year ever' in *New York Times*, 28 December, https://www.nytimes.com/2019/12/28/opinion/Sunday/2019-best-year-poverty.html, accessed 15 February 2020.

Legg, Angela M., Sara E. Andrews, Ho Huynh et al. (2015). 'Patients' anxiety and hope: Predictors and adherence intentions in an acute care context' in *Health expectations*, vol. 18, 3034–3043.

Lewis, Martyn (1993). 'Not my idea of good news' in *The Independent*, 26 April, https://www.independent.co.uk/voices/not-my-idea-of-good-news-at-the-end-of-a-week-of-horrifying-events-martyn-lewis-bbc-presenter-argues-1457539.html, accessed 24 March 2020.

Locke, John (1824). *Essay concerning human understanding*. London: John Bumpus.

Lomborg, Bjorn (2020). *False alarm: How climate change panic costs us trillions, hurts the poor, and fails to fix the planet*. London: Basic Books.

Macy, Joanna and Chris Johnstone (2012). *Active hope: How to face the mess we're in without going crazy*. Novato, CA: New World Library.

Mason, Will, Saeed Brasab, Brendan Stone et al. (n.d.). *Youth violence, masculinity and mental health*, University of Sheffield, https://www.sheffield.ac.uk/media/6787/download, accessed 25 March 2020.

Masten, Ann S. (2014). *Ordinary magic*: Resilience in development. New York: Guilford Press.

McCarthy, Cormack (2006). *The road*. New York: Alfred A. Knopf.

Meyler, Michael (2007). *Dictionary of Sri Lankan English*. Colombo: Michael Meyler.

Miyazaki, Hirokazu (2004). *The method of hope*. Stanford: Stanford University Press.

Moltmann, Jürgen (1967). *Theology of hope: On the ground and the implications of a Christian eschatology*. London: SCM Press.

Moltmann, Jürgen (2014). *Collected readings*, edited by Margaret Kohl. Minneapolis: Fortress Press.

Muers, Rachel (2015) *Testimony: Quakerism and theological ethics*. London: Student Christian Movement Press.

Nagel, Thomas (2008). 'The absurd' in *The meaning of life*, edited by E. D. Klemke and Steven Cahn. Oxford: Oxford University Press, 143–152.

New Economics Foundation (2020). *Framing the economy: How to win the case for a better system*, https://neweconomics.org/uploads/files/Framing-the-Economy-NEON-NEF-FrameWorks-PIRC.pdf, accessed 15 February 2020.

NPR (2019) 'Teen inspires youth demonstrations across Europe, demanding action on climate change', https://www.npr.org/2019/01/25/688793731/teen-inspires-youth-demonstrations-across-europe-demanding-action-on-climate-cha, accessed 11 March 2020.

Ondaatje, Michael (1982). *Running in the family*. New York: W. W. Norton.

Organisation for Economic Co-operation and Development (2020). 'Income inequality (indicator)', https://data.oecd.org/inequality/income-inequality.htm, accessed 25 March 2020.

Orwell, George (1949). 1984. London: Secker and Warburg.

Oxford Languages (2019). 'Word of the Year 2019', https://languages.oup.com/word-of-the-year/2019, accessed 11 March 2020.

Penn, William (1801). *No cross no crown: A discourse showing the nature and discipline of the Holy Cross of Christ*. London: W. Philips.

Pinker, Stephen (2011). *The better angels of our nature: The decline of violence in history and its causes*. London: Allen Lane.

Pinker, Stephen (2019). *Enlightenment now: The case for reason, science, humanism and progress*. London: Penguin.

Pyper, Hugh (2011). *The joy of Kierkegaard: Essays on Kierkegaard as a biblical reader*. Sheffield: Equinox.

Raleigh, Veena (2019). 'What is happening to life expectancy in the UK?', The King's Fund, https://www.kingsfund.org.uk/publications/whats-happening-life-expectancy-uk, accessed 17 March 2020.

Ridley, Matt (2010). *The rational optimist: How prosperity evolves*. London: Fourth Estate.

Robinson, Marilynne (2015). *The givenness of things*. London: Virago.

Rohr, Richard (2016). *Things hidden: Scripture as spirituality*. London: SPCK.

Rohr, Richard (2019). *The universal Christ: How a forgotten reality can change everything we see*. London: SPCK.

Rohr, Richard (n.d.). 'Advent with Richard Rohr', Franciscan Media, https://info.franciscanmedia.org/advent-with-richard-rohr-pillar, accessed 21 February 2020.

Rosling, Hans (2018). 'Good news at last: The world isn't as horrific as you think' in *The Guardian*, 11 April, https://www.theguardian.com/world/commentisfree/2018/apr/11/good-news-at-last-the-world-isnt-as-horrific-as-you-think, accessed 15 February 2020.

Russ, Mark (2019). *Towards a Quaker theology of hope: Postmodern Quaker eschatology through the lens of narrative* [MA dissertation], University of Nottingham.

Shakespeare, Tom and Alice Whieldon (2018). 'Sing Your Heart Out: Community singing as part of mental health recovery' in *Medical humanities*, vol. 44, 153–157.

Shakespeare, Tom, Anthony Mugeere, Emily Nyariki, and Joseph Simbaya (2019). 'Success in Africa: People with disabilities share their stories' in *African journal of disability*, vol. 8, 522.

Solnit, Rebecca (2016). *Hope in the dark: Untold histories, wild possibilities*. Edinburgh: Canongate.

Spufford, Francis (2012). *Unapologetic*. London: Faber and Faber.

Starke, Linda (1990). *Signs of hope: Working towards our common future*. Oxford: Oxford University Press.

UNAIDS (2019). 'Global HIV & AIDS statistics: 2019 fact sheet', https://www.unaids.org/en/resources/fact-sheet, accessed 19 March 2020.

Vanier, Jean (1999). *Becoming human*. London: Darton, Longman and Todd.

Ward, Madeleine (2019). 'The Christian Quaker: George Keith and the Keithian controversy' in *Quaker studies*, vol. 2, 1–101.

Webb, Darren (2007). 'Modes of hoping' in *History of the human sciences*, vol. 20, 65–83.

Wijesinghe, Manuka (2006). *Monsoons and potholes*. Colombo: Perera Hussein.

Williams, Rowan (2012). *Faith in the public square*. Bloomsbury: London.

Wittgenstein, Ludwig (1958). *Philosophical investigations*. Oxford: Blackwell.

World Commission on Environment and Development (1987). *Our common future*, https://www.are.admin.ch/are/en/home/sustainable-development/international-cooperation/2030agenda/un-_-milestones-in-sustainable-development/1987--brundtland-report.html, accessed 24 March 2020.

World Health Organization (2011). *World report on disability*, https://www.who.int/disabilities/world_report/2011/report/en, accessed 24 March 2020.

Lightning Source UK Ltd.
Milton Keynes UK
UKHW011838050820
367752UK00001B/93